MW00826697

Secrets of Combat Jujutsu Vol I

3rd Edition, 1st Printing

Published by:

Modern Bujutsu, Inc.
1811 NW 51 ST #2672
Fort Lauderdale, FL 33309 USA
www.miyamaryu.org

Warning

The material included in this book is for educational purposes and to promote continued self-defense training . The self-defense methods in this book are not guaranteed by the author to work or to be safe at any time.

In some situations, applications may not be warranted or allowable under local, state, or federal laws. No representations are made by theauthor regarding the appropriateness or legality of their use.

The techniques should be practiced under a licensed Miyama Ryu Instructor. Before trying any of these techniques, which could cause injury, you should consult a doctor. The author and Modern Bu-jutsu are not responsible if any such injury occurs.

Secrets of Combat Jujutsu Vol 1

3rd Edition, 1st Printing
Copyright (c) 1991, 1994, 2004 D'Arcy J. Rahming

ISBN #: 1-886219-07-9

Acknowledgements

Technical Consultant: Shinan Antonio Pereira, Miyama Ryu Founder
Publishing Consultant: Diane Skoss, Koryu Books
Editors: Jennifer Harris Baarman, Joye Ritchie Greene, Doug Utigard, Douglas Kryzan, Mark Russell, Erika Rahming
Summary Editor: Benita Rahming
Illustrations: Steven Taylor, Joe Garofalo
Uke: Arthur Steinberger, Dick Kazarian
Technical Editors:
Dai Shihan Demetrios Milliaressis, Dai Shihan William Duke,Shihan John Lewis, Shihan Omar Echavarria, Shihan Eileen Adams de Pereira, Sensei John Martin,Sensei Adam Orlov Sensei Daniel Wagner, Sensei Gamal Newry, Dr. John Rodgers, Melanie Lobosky, Rupert Adams, Julie Wagner, David Rahming,Sensei Don Koz
Cover designer: Kirkley Dean

Table of Contents

About the Author — Page 6
Foreword — Page 7
Introduction — Page 9
Lineage chart — Page 11
History of Combat Jujutsu — Page 12
History of Miyama Ryu — Page 15
A Talk with Shinan Pereira — Page 17
Miyama Ryu Heiho (Strategy and Tactics) — Page 19
Attitude in the Dojo — Page 22
Attitude in Training — Page 23
Attitude of theTori (Defender) — Page 24
Attitude of the Uke (Attacker) — Page 26
Unarmed Attacks — Page 28
Weapon Attacks — Page 29
Multiple Attacks — Page 30
Safety in the Dojo — Page 32
Sport? — Page 33
Taiso (Body Conditioning) — Page 34
Kamae (Posture and Attitude) — Page 39
Kiai Jutsu (The Spirit Shout) — Page 40
Owaza (the complete technique) — Page 42
Ukemi (Break Falls) — Page 43
Tai sabaki (body positioning) — Page 44
Atemi Waza (Striking Techniques) — Page 45
Kote Waza (Wrist Techniques) — Page 46
Kansetsu Waza (Joint Techniques) — Page 47
Nage Waza (Throwing Techniques) — Page 49
Shime Waza (Strangulation) — Page 51
Kyusho (Targeting Vital Areas) — Page 52
Maai (Combative Distance) — Page 55
Timing — Page 56

Table of Contents

Promotion Requirements for 6th Kyu Orange Belt   Page 57
Promotion Requirements for 5th Kyu Yellow Belt   Page 95
Promotion Requirements for 4th Kyu Green Belt   Page 124
Belt Tests and Promotion Requirements   Page 175
Rank and Promotion Procedures   Page 187
Index   Page 189

About the Author

D'Arcy Rahming is a Dai-Shihan (Head Master) of Miyama Ryu Combat Jujutsu. His martial arts credentials include Kaiden (9th degree Black Belt) in Miyama Ryu, 3rd Degree Black Belt in Okinawan Go Ju Ryu Karatedo, and 2nd degree Black Belt in Judo. He is also a dojo leader in Shindo Muso Ryu Jojutsu with the Pan American Jo Federation.

Rahming has over twenty five years experience in the martial arts, and has taught in several countries to thousands of people. Rahming has written 5 books and over 100 newspaper articles on self-protection. He has also served as a consultant to police and federal agencies.

Rahming currently teaches self-protection seminars and Miyama Ryu Jujutsu worldwide. He is an internationally renowned leader in the martial arts serving as President of the national Karate Federation and advisor to the national Judo Federation of the Bahamas. He is the owner of All-Star Family Karate with over 400 active students.

Foreword

I feel a great privilege to be a part of the Miyama Ryu Combat Jujutsu system. To write the foreword to this book is a tremendous honor and fills me with pride. I am grateful to the author for permitting me to make my contribution to the world of Jujutsu by being part of this valuable book.

To speak of Miyama Ryu Combat Jujutsu is to speak about Shinan Antonio Pereira (1922-1999). And to hear the name Dai Shihan D'Arcy Rahming is to be reminded of the Miyama Ryu Combat Jujutsu and Tremont School story. To make this book possible it had to be meticulously researched.

Professor Rahming is undoubtedly one of the best Jujutsu writers of this age. He has come to understand the real history, philosophy and spirit of this system and for this reason I deeply respect him and his dedication.

For many years I have trained in the art of Miyama Ryu Jujutsu and the Executive Board of the system recognizes that Professor Rahming is the only person with the capacity to write the official textbooks of our system.

This is a result of his teaching experience, contributions and support to the Ryu and especially the very close personal and confidential relationship he enjoyed with the founder of the system. He has been our best choice for expanding the secrets of Miyama Ryu Combat Jujutsu.

I consider this book easy to read and learn from for the general population and mandatory reading for all serious enthusiasts and practitioners of realistic self defense applications. It is therefore an essential addition to one's personal library, a work to be deeply studied by both teacher and student alike.

I highly recommend this book of Miyama Ryu Combat Jujutsu and hope that it will benefit those who seek the true essence of the martial arts.

Dai Shihan William Duke, MD, MPH
Executive Director
Miyama Ryu Combat Jujutsu
Dominican Republic

Introduction

Combat Jujutsu refers to a martial art used strictly for self-protection. It employs the use of empty hand as well as small weapons tactics. Combat Jujutsu was born on the battlefields of feudal Japan. To the Samurai Warrior, it was a secondary art to be used only when his long sword was unavailable or for their version of "street" defense. Its techniques were unknown to the general public.

Today this version of Combat Jujutsu is still a nearly lost art. Techniques are kept alive primarily by military and police organizations, usually in short courses on special tactics. Here too it is a secondary art, the primary weapons being firearms. In civilian practice there are only a few groups throughout the world who practice a street effective form of Combat Jujutsu.

In the 1990's a gladiator form of Jujutsu began to become popular, finding its rebirth in arenas across the world. These contests featured two highly skilled fighters competing against each other for prize money.

Popular magazines of the day coined the phrase Combat Jujutsu to refer to many of these styles. These gladiator arts have their place, as it is the nature of man to want to test his courage against other men.

However, while using the physical techniques of Combat Jujutsu, these gladiator contests have swayed from the original purpose of "street" defense which is: how not to be the victim of a violent crime.

Therefore, Miyama Ryu Combat Jujutsu includes not only the physical techniques, but the philosophy, mindset and psychological preparedness necessary to survive a violent encounter. Based on the research of Shinan Antonio Pereira, Shihan John Lewis and other members of the self-protection community I have formalized the systematic approach to the development of the Miyama Ryu. This approach I call Miyama Ryu Heiho (strategy) and it is the underlying theme of this series of Miyama Ryu books.

Classical Combat Jujutsu was developed by warriors for war. Today is a time of war - private, personal war. Murder, rape and other violent crimes against individuals sometimes fail to make the front page of most newspapers. Indeed, they sometimes even fail to make the newspaper at all except as part of a yearly statistic.

Miyama Ryu teaches how not to become one of these statistics. Most of the current literature in martial arts fails to address this true spirit. This first book serves as an introduction to Miyama Ryu. Miyama Ryu is one of the few remaining modern schools that are available to civilians.

At the time of this writing, the Ryu has been in existence for forty four years. During this time the quality of life for over 30,000 students worldwide has been enhanced by the positive virtues of Miyama Ryu.

I started this book many years ago as a collection of notes. It soon became a series of rough articles for my students and the students of my peers. Traditionally, the art has been passed down orally. When I began to train, I longed for a reference to supplement my training. Over the years I searched many bookstores for books on this elusive art. I concluded that there is very little credible literature on the art of Combat Jujutsu.

Many of the current books on martial arts address its modern derivatives. The problem with the majority of these texts is that their techniques have been modified either to a sport, an aesthetic dance, a cultural art or a platform to propagate confused mysticism.

Several changes have taken place since the last edition of this book was published. The original Founder Shinan Pereira has died, leaving his legacy to three highly competent successors, myself among them.

The Tremont School, which was the original Hombu Dojo, has closed its doors after 40 years of operation. There are many more schools of Miyama Ryu spread about the world and the original teachings threaten to become distorted unless some standard, as taught by the founder, is clearly documented.

This book is an improvement

over earlier editions for several reasons: My own experience level and understanding of the Miyama Ryu is different having been an instructor for over twenty years. Also, I have now taught Miyama Ryu in over five continents, to thousands of people of many different ages and of varying experience levels. Therefore, I bring more depth to these books as a teacher.

This physical technique in this new edition is organized around the minimum promotion requirements as taught by the founder Shinan Pereira. I stress the word minimum because each Miyama Ryu Instructor, depending on the perceived needs of his students may add additional techniques. But the techniques in this book are required for each belt level, no substitutes! They constitute the core of Miyama Ryu. Without them you are not practicing Miyama Ryu.

I have also included a section in each book on Sonota Waza (literally "those other things"). These are some of the techniques that were always taught but never formalized within the core curriculum.

It is my hope that these books will be an important step in preserving the rare treasure of Miyama Ryu.

Miyama Ryu Ju-jutsu (a historical perspective)

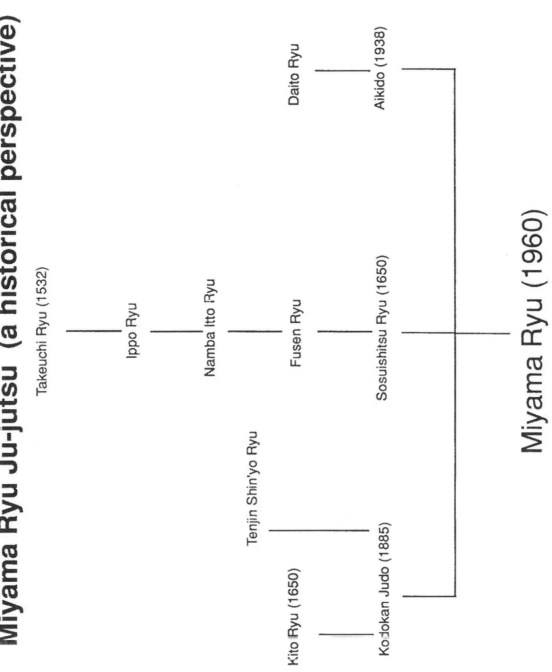

Takeuchi Ryu (1532)

Ippo Ryu

Namba Itto Ryu

Fusen Ryu

Sosuishitsu Ryu (1650)

Tenjin Shin'yo Ryu

Kito Ryu (1650)

Kodokan Judo (1885)

Daito Ryu

Aikido (1938)

Miyama Ryu (1960)

History of Combat Jujutsu

In 1877 Sokaku Takeda toured Japan, seeking enlightenment through the perfection of his fencing technique. This was the time just after the Samurai class had dissolved and the practice of swordsmanship was not well regarded.

One day Takeda passed a construction site where he was rudely stopped by one of the workers. The worker, his confidence bolstered by the presence of comrades, made disparaging remarks about Takeda's sword.

He then tried to wrench the sword from Takeda. In the struggle the construction worker was cut across the chest. His comrades were enraged. About fifty of them armed with various tools and bladed weapons surrounded Takeda and attempted to kill him.

Takeda drew his sword and retaliated. Any construction worker that came in range he cut down. By this time over three hundred workers had joined in the attack. The sheer numbers overwhelmed Takeda, but before they could slay him, the police arrived.

In all, Takeda had slain twelve men and wounded many others. When taken before the magistrate he was acquitted, but not before the magistrate aimed these words at him.

"Sokaku Takeda the time of the sword is over, put up your sword and learn Jujutsu."
* Sokaku Takeda was the teacher of Ueshiba, the Founder of Aikido.

The true origins of Combat Jujutsu are impossible to trace, though elements of the art can be found only in mythical stories and recorded fights dating back to 711 AD. Takenouchi founded one of the first Ryu that used Combat Jujutsu as the primary art, in 1532.

Legend has it, that while on a pilgrimage, Takenouchi trained and meditated intensely for several days. Finally, he collapsed from exhaustion. In his delirium he received a vision of a phantom warrior. This warrior taught him five techniques of immobilization, and the advantages of using short weapons over long ones.

Before the founding of the Takenouchi Ryu, combat techniques probably existed solely as a subordinate art to a major weapon system. Most modern Combat Jujutsu Ryus, including the Miyama Ryu, can trace their lineage directly back to techniques of the Takenouchi Ryu.

From the late 17th century to the middle of the 19th century, Combat Jujutsu was widely practiced by the Samurai. In peacetime and with the dissolution of the warrior class, however, Jujutsu lost its emphasis on combat.

The Koryu (old traditions) has survived to a certain extent and has found its way to the western world. Strict adherents of the Koryu insist that in order to understand it, one must either go to Japan, absorb the culture, or study with someone who has spent a considerable amount of time in Japan.

Obviously the conditions of street defense and combat have changed; therefore the Koryu can no longer be termed Combat Jujutsu. Many of the Koryu teachers became bonesetters, as they were well practiced from the injuries that occurred in the Dojo.

Unfortunately, many more used their skills to put on fake wrestling shows for public amusement, or to become gangsters. For these reasons, Combat Jujutsu lost reputation and was soon regarded as an art practiced by undesirables and thugs.

An aesthetic type of Jujutsu did survive. The now-banned Samurai taught it to commoners, who modified it into a more artistic and graceful form. Combat Jujutsu has found its way to the Western world in one of two forms: the Koryu Jujutsu adapted to modern combative situations, or the eclectic approach of combining the arts of Karate, Judo, and Aikido in a modern context.

It is important to note that there are several people in the world today who believe that if you study Judo and Karate, achieve Black Belt rankings in both, and then combine them, you have created a Combat Jujutsu Ryu.

Keep in mind that true modern combat teachers design their systems from actual combat experience, as well as an in-depth knowledge of the traditional arts.

These arts are not a hodgepodge of ideas thrown together; rather, they flow from years of intensive study. In order to have a realistic modern Combat Jujutsu there must be some unifying principle. In Miyama Ryu that principle is: How not to become the victim of a violent crime.

Shinan Antonio Pereira and Aikido Founder O'Sensei Ueshiba, Tokyo, Japan, August 1962

History of Miyama Ryu

In 1942 Antonio Pereira, a young American soldier, was participating in a hand-to-hand demonstration. When ordered to punch one of the instructors in the face, he complied, only to find himself whipped around into a chokehold.

During World War II, Pereira learned as much as he could about specialized combat methods. He continued to experiment and practice with the techniques, refining them sometimes under life and death situations.

After the war, his warrior's quest for additional knowledge took him to many schools in search of martial prowess. In 1950 he began a formal study of judo with the Lefcoker brothers. He began to research how victims of crime were attacked and devise methods of practical defense.

In 1960 he opened a martial arts school on Tremont Avenue, in the South Bronx, New York. He called his rough-and-tumble method of fighting Combato. But the puzzle was still not complete. In 1962 he embarked on a journey to Japan. His plan was to study from the source, and perhaps to gain a better sense of the martial principles.

As he observed the practice at the Aiki Kai (Aikido school), Pereira recognized similarities to what he had been doing all along. Pereira set out to learn the more refined methods. His fierce resolve and dedication won him many honors. Among them

were, a teaching certificate from O'Sensei Ueshiba (son of the founder of Aikido), and a Ni dan in Judo from the Kodokan (the birth place of Judo).

Pereira returned to the United States and resumed teaching at the Tremont School. Periera would later earn a San Mokuroku in Sosuishitsu Ryu Jujutsu a Koryu (Jujutsu) from the then Headmaster Professor Shitama.

Knowing that the Western life style and philosophy differs from the Eastern, he adapted the physical techniques and mind set of the Samurai Warrior to the culture of the dangerous streets of the modern, urban South Bronx.

In effect, he created one of the few combat methods suited for today's streets. He combined elements of Judo, Aikido, Koryu Jujutsu, Karate, Boxing, and the less organized, but no less effective element of Western street-style fighting.

In 1964 he formalized the name of his eclectic method Miyama Ryu Jujutsu, which means School of the Three Mountains in English, or Tremont in French. This was the avenue on which the school was located.

In 1973 Pereira researched the classical ranking system of Japanese systems. He decided to use the ranking structure and nomenclature of the Japanese martial arts, both classical and modern. He took the title of

Shinan, which means originator.

Shinan Pereira died in 1999 and with him the era of Tremont as the center of Miyama Ryu came to an end. Miyama Ryu has branched out from the tough streets of the South Bronx to several countries in several continents. Not only is it taught to civilians, but it has been used in the design of courses for United States Federal agents, taught at police and law enforcement academies across the world and is still being refined today by a cadre of Kaidens (Senior Instructors) and three Dai-Shihans who are the successors to this dynamic and important art.

A Talk with Shinan Pereira

November 27, 1922 - July 16, 1999

In order to understand Miyama Ryu it is necessary to understand Shinan Pereira's thinking in its formulation. Here he tells of some of his philosophy in his own words. This interview was conducted at Northwestern University in 1987 by the author. Hopefully you will gain insights into the true purpose and structure of the Miyama Ryu.

What actions inspired the formulation of Miyama Ryu?

This started in the back of my mind in 1943 during the war. When I got back in '45, I looked for, but I couldn't find anything that would suit me. Not that I was particular. In the late '50's I found something. Then I started to view it from a different perspective. What does it do for me? I told myself at the time, "I am number one," and each and every one of you should say that to yourself. You are number one.

Now, when I started teaching, my technique was called Combato. You can imagine; they said to me, "Mr. Pereira, if you keep teaching in this fashion you'll never have any students." My answer was, "I don't know anything else." Which was the truth. It was horrible. When I threw a man, I wanted to throw him into hell. Those who stayed with me persevered. At this time, there is only one left of the original crew - Shihan Klett.

Now when I decided to formulate something, make this my life, I went to Japan. I went to Japan so I could get this puzzle in my head together. Finally, I walked into the Aiki Kai.

At that time you had to be recommended; you couldn't just say, "Hey, I'm Joe Blow from New York, take me in." When I walked in I said to myself, "I've been doing this all along," not knowing what I was doing. What the Aiki Kai did was put this thing in the right perspective.

And then of course the Judo Institute, I was there for six months training every single day. I lost 35 lbs. When I came out of the Judo Institute I was a second-degree black belt. When I came there they said "What are you?" I said, "I'm nothing; you tell me what I am."

The training in Japan was very hard, very demanding. From 6:30 a.m. to 8:30 a.m. I would train at the Aiki Kai. From 9:30 a.m. - 12:00 p.m. I would train with Sensei Tohei. At 12:00 p.m. I would go with my Judo Sensei and we would start to make the rounds at the high schools. From 3:00 p.m. to 9:00 p.m. we would train at the Kodokan. This happened five days a week except during special training when it occurred seven days a week.

When I got back, I changed the name of the style. The School is on Tremont Avenue, so I called my method Miyama Ryu which means Tremont... Nothing esoteric.

Why did you originate Miyama Ryu as opposed to teaching the classical methods?

If you saw Jujutsu in Japan, we as Americans, would laugh. People from the South Bronx would "Ha ha!" and say, "What the devil are they doing?" Their ways are not our ways. Their system of training is very ritualistic.

So I said let me take out these nonsensical things and put it in the form of a 'blow is a blow.' And this is what we have. But when I went through these actions I tried to cut out the very serious parts that could hurt you severely during training.

Why then do we practice Classical Kata at advanced levels?

Only at advanced levels can you understand the true meaning of Kata. In Miyama Ryu up to the 1st Kyu rank everything is bang bang. Then at Okuiri you begin to become refined through the practice of Kata.

How would you describe the use of your voice as an instructor?

Very strong, very forceful. By the tone and pitch it sometimes portrays anger and anxiety, sometimes caressing. If I offend with one word I must caress with the other.

Why use the Menkyo system of ranking as opposed to the modern Dan system?

The reason why I took my people out of the numbers racket was because everybody was a seventh or eighth dan or master ninth. Even Kano himself didn't have a grade. Uyeshiba didn't have a grade; the father of Karatedo didn't have a grade. In the Miyama Ryu system I don't have a grade. I have a title, Shinan, meaning 'originator.' When I'm gone my belt color will be buried with me.

Through a Japanese acquaintance Minoru Morita we put everything together. The system that we have has a possibility of eight grades but I chose only four: Okuiri, Mokuroku, Menkyo and Kaiden.

What advice do you have for current and future instructors of the art?

I refined as much as I could. But the refinement comes from each and every one of your personalities not only me. Each and every one of you can contribute something to the system.

But you must stay by the basics of the system, do not divert from them. It serves no purpose to modify the basics as all the pieces of the puzzle have been carefully put together.

Shinan Pereira, WW II Combat Veteran, 1943 - 1945

Miyama Ryu Heiho (Strategy and Tactics)

"For me, the real value of Miyama Ryu Combat Jujutsu is in its defenses against multiple attackers. Most systems that I have studied, (if they deal with multiple attackers at all), focus on developing speed and strength. With Miyama Ryu, there was a particular pattern to follow. The emphasis was on strategies.

These strategies served me well on many occasions. Up to the time of this writing, because of my job and where I live, I have been attacked by two or more opponents five times and single attackers six times. Because of Miyama Ryu training I was able to control my fear and other emotions, avoid serious injury and survive the encounters.

As a Miyama Ryu Instructor I have tried very hard to pass on the concept that strategy is just as (if not more important) than skill.

I thank the Shinan (and God) every day for developing a system that has saved my life so many times and was not contaminated by changes made in the dojo that was disconnected from actual combat."

— Shihan Curtis M. Inniss, Florida, USA

To successfully defend himself, the warrior was able to quickly analyze the assault, prepare a plan of action with alternatives and, immediately gain control of the situation. Miyama Ryu Heiho is the method by which students with no experience in actual fighting are able to quickly become effective in not being the victim of a violent crime.

Miyama Ryu Heiho has five stages. These stages are:
1) Mind-set,
2) Scenario based training,
3) Awareness and threat assessment
4) Response
5) Analysis and feedback.

Of course these are general guidelines and although they are taught in a hierarchical manner, each stage is a field of study within itself. There are natural crossovers between various stages.

The first stage is developing the correct mind-set . There are things that you must determine in your mind even before an attack has begun. For example, you should know under which conditions you would resist an armed attacker before facing the scenario, because at the time of the attack, hesitation and doubt could cost you your life.

As Shihan John Lewis would say, "Draw the line in the sand now!" Also included in this stage is an understanding of the bad guy's psychology. This is essential because it allows you to analyze his actions and prepare the appropriate response.

The second stage is scenario based training. This is where most modern martial arts begin and end. These are the practical techniques needed to defeat an adversary. The techniques illustrated in this book are examples of scenario based training.

While these techniques are essential to the Miyama Ryu, they are not *the* Miyama Ryu. If you only understand the physical techniques, you will have missed the whole point. As Shinan would say, "there are only so many ways to twist an arm."

The third stage is awareness and threat assessment. You must become aware of your surroundings and environment. You must learn how to make yourself less likely to be chosen as a victim just by your sense of presence. Included in this stage is violence de-escalation and retreating from danger before it even occurs.

Threat assessment goes hand in hand with awareness. In a violent confrontation you can count on attacks from more than one adversary. You must attempt to identify potential adversaries and accomplices. Sometimes potential adversaries are obvious; for example, you are involved in a car accident and two adversaries jump out of the automobile and attempt to assault you. At other times, an accomplice may be hiding behind a doorway.

There is also the concept that you will be judged by how you are perceived by others in a modern society. In addition to identifying the adversaries, you must identify other potential threats. How is the adversary holding his hands? Does it look like he is carrying a concealed weapon? These are the types of questions that may save your life.

Miyama Ryu Jujutsu training provides solutions to many of these situations. For example, the basic defense techniques against a knife thrust to the stomach involve the defender turning 180 degrees, which allows him to see other potential assailants.

Using your environment is vital to reacting to threats. Identifying potential exits or areas that you can use for cover may allow you to avert danger in many instances.

Additionally, the environment provides us with a myriad of weapons ranging from items as innocuous as a ballpoint pen, which can be used to attack vital areas, or a weapon as obvious as a baseball bat.

The Miyama Ryu unarmed techniques easily incorporate these environmental weapons. The overriding objective of Combat Jujutsu is to survive a violent encounter; so a response such as smashing someone over the head with a chair is as acceptable as using a joint-locking technique.

Although Miyama Ryu Jujutsu exponents train in the classical weaponry used by the samurai warriors and modern weapons carried by street thugs, carrying a device used specifically for a weapon is discouraged. In a life-and-death situation you will become psychologically dependent on your weapon.

For example, if you have to defend yourself and you are carrying a knife, you will attempt to use this knife, even if it is not your best option.

Whereas, if you picked up a chair to strike the adversary and this strategy was thwarted, chances are that you would not worry too much about retrieving it, since you only used it because it was convenient.

The ability to adjust your focus is an integral part of a successful self-defense strategy. When you engage an adversary, your attention is focused on defeating him. In some circumstances it is necessary to focus on the adversary. For example, if you were attacked with a night stick to the side of the head, you would attack the arm and not the stick.

When you are finished with one adversary you must switch your focus automatically to the others. If you do not adjust quickly, you will develop tunnel vision. During a multiple-man attack, tunnel vision could have fatal consequences.

An essential part of Miyama Ryu Heiho is to understand and utilize the complete technique. The complete technique consists of: an evasion or block of the initial attack; a strike to loosen up the adversary and take his focus away from his intended attack; a major technique such as a throw, joint-lock or choke; and a finishing strike or ground control to immobilize the attacker. The ground control is

sometimes preceded by a strike if the attacker is still active and you want to control him.

Response is the fourth stage of the Miyama Ryu Heiho. The Miyama Ryu makes extensive use of testimonials from individuals who have actually applied the techniques in real life encounters. There are countless Miyama Ryu testimonials from individuals with the experience of a few lessons to individuals with years of experience.

Many of these stories come from law enforcement officers as well as civilians. The various Chief Instructors analyze these actions. This is not a form of second guessing the incident, rather an attempt to recreate the incident and its environment with a view to improving teaching methods and the curriculum of the Ryu.

Because you may be judged by how your actions are perceived, it is important that you are aware of the self-defense laws that govern your jurisdiction. Miyama Ryu Heiho does not offer legal advice but seeks to make you aware that this is a consideration in technique selection and the level of force used.

The fifth stage of Miyama Ryu Heiho is the analysis of the action and feedback. The entire situation is analyzed with a view toward whether it could have been avoided or if thoughts and actions were best choices.

This is done by the Chief Instructor at the various schools

and can lead to a change in the emphasis of the training or teaching method of the student or of the entire Dojo.

Feedback is very important to both teachers and students, and the instructor should never take a "you should have done this" type attitude. This is a time for listening on the Instructor's part.

Enhancements and modifications are also a part of this stage. The Miyama Ryu curriculum is evaluated and if necessary, modified to add new scenarios, refine techniques or add new techniques.

While any individual instructor can add techniques to his school's curriculum, modification of the official Miyama Ryu curriculum as contained in this series of books is done at the Dai Shihan level with the help of their technical committees.

Attitude in the Dojo

"While walking home I was approached by two men in their early twenties. One of them asked me for a cigarette and I told him I didn't have any and I started to walk away. About half a block away I was pushed against a wall by one of the men. I turned towards him and the other one grabbed me from behind in the #1 chest grab. I threw him into the oncoming attacker with Aiki #1.

He landed on his back and head and was knocked unconscious. The other came at me with a roundhouse right, I blocked it with the Taisabaki #2 and threw him with Ippon Seionage and came down with Shuto to the face. I left the two of them on the floor and walked away. The whole incident took less than a minute and all I suffered was a scraped elbow."

—Aaron Grossman, New York, USA

In Miyama Ryu Combat Jujutsu there are no hidden techniques. From the first day the student faces the reality of the street. All techniques are fighting techniques, the technique that you learn the first day as a white belt still has value 20 years later. What makes a technique more advanced is the practitioner's ability to perform its timing and dynamics under stressful situations.

There is a tendency among contemporary martial artists to embrace one of two extreme attitudes towards their arts. The first attitude is to overemphasize ritual in the name of tradition. Under the guise of tradition, supposed experts try to create an atmosphere that makes students afraid to question anything that is taught. This version of tradition usually resembles a bad Samurai movie.

The second popular attitude is to call all tradition "a classical mess." This attitude claims to foster creativity, but more often it fosters a slack environment. It is common to see individuals, with a few years training, calling themselves masters. In some unexplainable way they must believe that they have surpassed their teachers.

Combat Jujutsu has no masters, only disciples. It is not the work of mystics, but rather a military science involving principles of leverage, strength and anatomical knowledge. Combine these physical factors with the psychological preparedness needed to defeat a determined adversary, and the result is a devastatingly real fighting science.

The modern dojo is not a temple. Zen, Taoism and Buddhism have no place in the training hall. Ideas from these philosophies may help to strengthen a fighter's resolve. But other fighters may find an equal support from nonreligious sources. Religion is not a part of the training.

The classical schools' strict formality in practice was based on respect. This attitude carries through in the modern tradition. Respect for teachers, present and past, is important. Respect for training partners and the training environment is equally important. In many military organizations respect is observed by a salute; in business, by a handshake; and in Miyama Ryu, by a bow.

Attitude in the Training

"In my 20 years of leading a fugitive squad for a probation department, the techniques taught to me directly by Shinan Pereira, have kept me safe and out of harm. There are no more effective techniques for the apprehension of fugitives."

— Shihan Miguel Ibarra, New York, USA

In the Koryu (classical schools of combat), techniques were practiced in a very formal manner. Most training was conducted through two man Kata (prearranged exercises). Trainees adapted an unquestioning attitude.

Modification of any techniques within the Kata was unheard of, for they had been developed in actual combat. Teachers believed that peacetime tampering would lead to unreliable techniques, resulting in the death of practitioners.

When Samurai fought there were three possible outcomes: the Samurai's death, his adversary's death or a mutual slaying. Against an equally skilled adversary, this implied a two-thirds chance of dying. Consistent technique seemed the best shield against such long odds.

In modern times the conditions of war have changed. Techniques can be updated through the lessons of actual experiences: attempted muggings, attempted assaults and police work.

Also, for the civilian who practices Combat Jujutsu, killing is rarely necessary, even though it may be the intention of your adversary. Greater emphasis is placed on immobilizing an adversary after stopping his attack.

The training methods of the Koryu are difficult to apply to the Western world. The Samurai warrior spent most of his life perfecting techniques that he could use in a life or death situation.

There are few of us who have the motives or the time that a Samurai warrior brought to his training. Most modern practices last between one and two hours and meet two to three times a week. This is usually the only time that students can train under the supervision of a qualified instructor.

Training only twice a week is not enough. You should spend as much time practicing at home as at the dojo. This practice may take the form of 10 minutes of pantomiming techniques in the morning and at convenient times during the day. There is no need for formal practice attire. Jujutsu must become a natural part of your life, not just something you do a couple of times a week.

Train yourself mentally as well as physically. One exercise is to read the newspaper of any major city and imagine yourself in a similar situation as the victim of a particular crime. Could you have defended yourself or possibly avoided the incident entirely? Use your imagination to experiment with the techniques at home.

In the dojo and at home, techniques should be practiced from both sides. It is likely that real attacks will not occur exactly as you practiced in class. Do homework on every technique. Experiment with different angles of attack, always keeping in mind that they must be applied with a serious attitude.

Attitude of the Tori (Defender)

" I was performing a tour of 6:00 am to 2:30 pm...I was assigned to red light overtime. I positioned my marked police vehicle near the intersection of Rosedale Ave and the Cross Bronx Expressway Service Road. I just pulled over a vehicle at approximately. 11:10 a.m. for going through the red light, it was occupied by two males... approximately 20 years old.

I approached the vehicle to ask for the driver's license, registration and insurance card. The guys were looking around to see if I had a partner (I didn't) at that point they both jumped out of the vehicle.

I immediately stopped and looked to see if any one of them had pulled a gun or any other weapon...they didn't. The driver threw a looping right punch to my head which I quickly blocked...returning a front kick to his groin and then threw him with an Osotogari at that point the passenger attempted to grab me from behind his arms across my chest...I elbowed him and stepped to the side and did Sankyo (wrist technique).

Later on during the arrest process one of the detectives discovered that these guys were members of a gang and they were attempting to take my 9mm as a trophy...they went to jail and I now enjoy my monthly pension checks."

—*Shihan Joe Martinez, New York, USA*

As the Tori, put yourself in the mindset of an actual defender. That may sound obvious, but there is a torrent of emotions that are present during an attack that are difficult to duplicate in a class setting.

If you treat the training as a sport or just another form of physical exercise, the techniques will not work in combat. There are numerous health benefits attached to the training, but self-preservation is the primary purpose. Never forget the seriousness behind an attack.

To avoid anticipating an attack and being faked out, try to remain calm at all times. Take in your entire surroundings and control your emotions. This controlled state is perhaps the most important aspect of the practice, and the most difficult concept to attain.

To react efficiently, you must be a whirlwind of concentrated fury for an instant, and then return to a calm center between attacks. Keep in mind that there is probably more than one attacker. Uncontrolled emotion leads to tunnel vision, which is undoubtedly a major reason highly skilled fighters sometimes lose in street confrontations.

Be aware that you are also responsible for the safety of your training partner. How many of us have trained with an overly enthusiastic partner who seems very insensitive to our pain? The practice is a game of give and take. During class time, injury is our only real enemy.

As the defender, you must constantly ask yourself three questions: What is my target? What is my distance? What is my timing?

Targeting comes with continued practice. Every technique must have a distraction, misdirection or an Atemi (strike). Without this, it is unlikely that any major disabling technique such as a choke or wrist breaking can occur.

You determine the distance of the attack. In class the attack is, generally started from one step away. On the street, if someone you perceive as hostile steps too close, you would either move away or ask them firmly to step back.

Though you may have made an incorrect assumption, it is far easier to live with that, than to die from a knife wound because you did not have time to react.

Practicing Combat Jujutsu involves teamwork, the spirit of cooperation. If you are the Tori and learning the drills, your timing should be about one-quarter the speed of an actual attack. Give your partner a chance to set up for the fall, particularly if he lacks experience.

In Miyama Ryu you must take into consideration, your age and health as well as the age and health of the individual(s) with whom you are working; then work at the appropriate pace. For example, if the falling surface is not ideal for practice, then only practice to the point of throwing (uchikomi) without actually practicing the fall.

Constant practice of attacks will reduce the shock when a real attack occurs. The best time to make mistakes is in the presence of your instructor, so put your ego and pride aside and do not be afraid to make them. Over my years of training I have "died" many times in the dojo. I will continue to "die" - so that I might live if I am attacked in the street.

Attitude of the Uke (Attacker)

"In 1996 I moved to Colorado where I became employed in a county jail. I was employed at this jail for 3 1/2 years. During my employment, I had many physical altercations with uncooperative inmates.

On every occasion I was able to subdue the combative inmate without causing injury to them or myself. I was always able to do so in a very safe and effective way using the techniques I learned in the Miyama Ryu system. My co-workers and supervisors always requested my assistance when a potentially dangerous situation arose."

— Sean Harper, Colorado, USA

The Uke's role is to prepare the Tori, mentally and physically, to survive an actual street-attack. I have had the displeasure of witnessing several demonstrations in which the Uke executes an attack without true injurious intent. While the defender usually reacts with plausible techniques, both participants are deceiving each other. If the Uke does not attack with intent in class, he is doing the defender a grave disservice. The defender now believes that he possesses some skill. Unfortunately, that skill is untested.

Knowledge of a technique is not enough. Proper attacks are vital in developing the right timing and dynamics.

This rule of intent applies even when you are first learning the technique. During the familiarization period, the technique should be practiced totally without Uke resistance. The attack should begin at about a quarter of actual speed. As you become more familiar with the technique, increase the speed in quarter increments.

Executing a training attack requires mental discipline. You must forget yourself for the moment and become a vicious adversary, yet you must maintain control to avoid injuries. During rapid order drills in which both Uke and Tori are well versed, attacks must be accurate and at full speed and power.

Mock weapons should be used, such as padded clubs and wooden knives. Handle the mock weapons with the respect that you would give a live blade. Working with live blades is only for very advanced levels. One of the premises of the art is that you must be prepared to be injured during a real fight. Remember also that the defender, your partner, probably has to go to work in the morning.

An Uke must learn to react once the defender has begun his counterattack. If a counter punch is aimed at your head, simulate being struck. The Uke's role is one of nonresistance during the major technique. On the street a takedown or joint-breaking technique would rarely be applied to an adversary who is still able to resist. Loosening up techniques, (which will be explained in the striking section), are always applied first.

Other martial arts practitioners sometimes perceive Jujutsu to be impractical. A commonly heard criticism is that "nobody is going to stand there and let you do all those techniques to them." They are absolutely correct; if the Uke simply throws a punch then patiently waits for a technique to be applied.

Combat Jujutsu is extremely dynamic, but without an aggressive Uke, it quickly loses its flavor. Effective Jujutsu techniques work off the premise that the adversary reacts to being countered.

In Miyama Ryu the techniques take into account the intelligence of the attacker. Questions such as, "Will the attacker attempt to withdraw his weapon after his initial attack?" are considered.

Another factor is that during combat, the adversary will generally throw a strong primary attack. The Miyama Ryu Jujutsu techniques capitalize on openings created by this aggressive strategy. In the best of circumstances the adversary is finished within a few seconds, regardless of his fighting prowess.

Many students become discouraged when a technique works in class but does not seem to work when applied to a friend. Be aware that the techniques are more than just a series of movements.

The mind-set behind the action is critical. The techniques are not designed for play or to be done halfheartedly. If you are not prepared to hurt this friend, then do not try the techniques. As a general rule, do not train with people who are not practitioners themselves.

Unarmed Attacks

"One morning at 1 a.m. I was walking home after parking my car on a side street and was suddenly attacked by two assailants. The first man attempted to attack me from behind by placing his right arm forcefully around my neck, (using mug #1).

At the same time his accomplice stepped out in front of me attacking me simultaneously, (obviously in accordance with their prepared plan). Naturally as I have been taught, I countered the mug #1 with throw #1 in a mug hold, strike grab and then throw over the right shoulder.

Assailant number 2 was coming at me with a looping right. I countered with Taisabaki #2 and used Koshi Guruma leaving the two attacker's unconscious."

— Gilbert Merced, New York, USA

Punches, slaps, shoves, kicks and hits constitute unarmed striking attacks. Defenses are taught from the first day through the Taisabaki.

With mugs and rear body grabs, the adversary grabs you from behind. You are already in serious trouble for two reasons. First, if he was able to grab you, he is probably also able to hit or stab you from behind. Second, there is probably more than one adversary.

A front body grab also indicates a bad situation. It means that the adversary has gotten through your Taisabaki defenses and is now intent on throwing you to the ground or crushing you into submission.

Body grabs and mugs are natural extensions of each other. Mugs deal with a rear attack on the neck. With body grabs from the rear, attacks are defined as above the elbows, below the elbows and under the arms. Front body grabs are described in a similar fashion. Practice these techniques diligently. Keep in mind that while these actions are not as glamorous as facing a knife, they are no less important and could make all the difference when facing a streetwise attacker.

Practice these techniques from all angles and in various multiple man situations. You must be able to quickly react, and position yourself before the next attacker comes.

Weapon Attacks

"John, a student of ours who had been in the club for only a couple of quarters, attended an apartment party that turned ugly. John got into a verbal altercation with another individual over the fact that John had spoken to a particular woman at the party.

The individual walked away and John went back to mingling. A moment later John heard some commotion and turned to see that the individual he had been arguing with was coming at him with a steak knife that he had retrieved from the kitchen.

"The offender attempted to thrust the knife into John's stomach. John performed a rear oblique step with a butterfly block. The tip of the blade did slightly cut John's stomach (later requiring 5 stitches), but John secured the offender's wrist and performed a pivot with Kote Gaeshi wrist break.

As the offender's wrist snapped, he fell to the floor and John struck him in the face, breaking his nose and driving his head into the floor."

—Sensei Adam Orlov, Illinois, USA

When facing a knife, expect to be cut. When facing a club, expect to be hit. This is the basic premise of fighting an armed adversary. Under no circumstances do you ever want to take a full stab to any body part. However, expect to receive glancing cuts. Being stabbed produces a numbing feeling and may very well take you out of the fight. A nonfatal slash may not even be noticed until the end of the fight. Although the techniques are called knife defenses they defend against any edged weapon, including broken glass, screwdrivers, and razors. Similarly, club defenses work against pipes, umbrellas, canes or any blunt weapon. In this book the techniques employed against armed attackers are striking, joint locking, wrist turning, and major throws. With the proper entry all are interchangeable.The key to facing an armed attacker lies with the Taisabaki.

The best defense against an attack is not to be there. So, in each movement, the defender takes the endangered body part out of harm's way as the adversary tries to slash the student's face, the student will block with his arm and move his face forward slightly. If the block fails, the defender is hit with the side of the hand as opposed to being sliced with the edge of the knife.

Edged and bludgeoned weapons are very common in society. Daily newspapers tell horrific stories of victims being stabbed or bludgeoned dozens of times before dying. Frequently when individuals have been stabbed or bludgeoned, their hands are wrecked with defensive wounds. The point is that putting up your hands is simply not enough to protect against a determined adversary. Moving your body is the key.

The constant theme of the following techniques is that the closer you are to an adversary, the safer you are. A club in the hands of an unskilled individual is useless at close distances. A knife also loses its effectiveness, as the adversary needs room to be able to put power behind the slash or cut. Fending the adversary off with strikes alone is a losing strategy, because before long the defender will be trading a cut for a strike.

If you successfully disarm your adversary, you can use his own weapon against him. Another advantage is that the adversary is tied to his weapon psychologically. Once the weapon has been dislodged, the adversary quickly loses his confidence. This is another vital concept: the adversary's attention is on his weapon while the defender's attention is on the adversary.

Multiple Attacks

" I was coming home from work on Palm Sunday, when three guys approached me two blocks from my house. They stopped me and one said, "I want your money and your jacket." One of them kept saying "Don't do this man we're gonna get busted." I started to walk away from them after I said I wasn't going to give them anything. One of them grabbed me in an upper chest grab as the other two ran in front of me. I threw the one who grabbed me. When he hit the ground, he must have hit his head on the concrete because I put my hand under his head to lift it up to strike his face when I noticed blood on it.

"The first guy, who asked for money and my jacket, took a switchblade from his back pocket, held it out and opened it. I guess to try and scare me. He then gave me a stomach thrust. I used basic. When I went to give him Kotegaeshi, he stiffened his arm up. I gave him a kick and applied the Kotegaeshi harder. I heard a sound but didn't know what it was at first. When I went to bring him down to the face his wrist rotated and he screamed. I realized what the sound was I heard. I had broken his wrist.

I looked at the guy who said they were going to get busted. He stood right where he was and said that it was cool. I picked up the knife threw it down the sewer and ran. I ran around the block to my building and went into the back door.

When I reached home I realized that I didn't think of the techniques. I just did them."

— J. Chianese, New York, USA

In general, a criminal will choose a target that he feels he can overcome with as little resistance as possible. The criminal will seldom act without the security of superior strength, superior weapons or superior numbers.

During a multiple attack, awareness is the most important factor. In a Karate or Judo match, you direct your attention solely to defeating your opponent and ignore the crowd. In a life or death situation, you can never ignore the crowd. The basic body positioning techniques are flexible, so the defender can move to any position regardless of the second attacker's direction.

Kotegaeshi, Kansetsuwaza and major throwing, force the defender to see 360 degrees as he turns to make his technique. This is not by accident. All of the actions were designed under life and death situations and would be less effective if they did not include this principle.

Defending against multiple attacks demands a minimal amount of footwork. The condition of the ground you stand on is known by the mere fact that you are standing. If you must fight near electric tracks or on ice, one step in the wrong direction could mean death.

In multiple attacks, the first assailant must be brought down very hard. To turn the fight into a wrestling match could cost you your life, because the attacker's accomplices can kill you even if you are more skilled than the initial attacker. A strong response to the first attacker gives accomplices second thoughts as they realize that they have chosen the wrong target.

It is improbable that two or more attackers will attack at exactly the same time; they would get in each other's way. A carefully planned attack might occur almost simultaneously. For example, one attacker might grab and the other stab. The key to the defense is to move the initial attacker's body into the path of his accomplice(s).

Major techniques should be utilized. Many martial arts do not advocate grappling with an individual during a multiple attack believing that a series of well placed blows will incapacitate the attackers. This is only partially true. Defeating adversaries solely through multiple strikes is unlikely. This strategy is too time consuming and does not give the defender the advantage of directing one adversary into the path of another. In addition, multiple strikes dissipate the defender's energy too quickly. Against multiple assailants this could mean death.

This does not mean that strikes are not vital in multiple

assailant defense. It does mean that strikes must fit into the pattern of the full technique. A similar argument could be presented against throwing or joint locking since these actions will not work individually without proper loosening-up techniques. When a strike is followed by a throw or joint lock, the attacker is thrown to the ground injured.

Never use ground strikes or controls; this will take you away from the multiple attack situation. It is far better to face a semi-injured attacker a second time than to be clubbed to death while trying to administer a coup de grace on the first attacker.

Safety in the Dojo

"In the dojo injury is our only enemy!"

— *Sensei Shunichi Namba, Illinois, USA*

There are many approaches to teaching Miyama Ryu. But there is one constant...any student not willing to abide by the Chief Instructor's rules should not be allowed to practice under any circumstances.

One of the primary objectives of any legitimate teacher should be to provide a safe practice. In Miyama Ryu we practice against realistic attacks using full contact defenses. Mock weapons are also utilized to enhance the level of training and realism. The workout is very spirited and to an outside observer, the sight of bodies flying everywhere may appear very violent and uncontrolled.

But the reality is that the workout is extremely controlled and in a properly supervised dojo injuries are very rare. The control begins with the Sensei (instructor). In the dojo, the Sensei's word is the law. He assumes complete responsibility for every person on the mat.

The command of "Stop!" means that all action in the dojo must come to an immediate halt. When the instructor addresses the class, all students must pay complete attention. This level of authority is necessary because if someone is in danger of being injured, the instructor must be able to correct the situation immediately.

In some cases during class, the Sensei may request more experienced students to supervise sub-groups within the same class. However the Sensei is still the ultimate authority in the dojo.

The senior student's role is to assist the Sensei. In the case of a Sensei's absence, one senior student must assume the authority of Sensei. This is a source of contention because in many Dojos there are often students of the same rank with similar time in grade.

However, for safety reasons, when the Sensei is absent, this senior student must have the same authority as the Sensei, even over his peers. This person should be designated ahead of time by the Sensei, or if this is not possible the person should be determined amongst the senior students before class begins.

If there are personality clashes, and for whatever reason one of the senior students cannot abide by the rules of the primary senior, then he should exclude himself from the practice and not participate at all.

Safety in the dojo makes for a better learning experience for all. People from all walks of life practice Miyama Ryu and no one comes to the Dojo if he feels he will be injured.

Sport?

The two combatants stand glaring at one another. Their bodies are rigid; fists clenched awaiting the referee's commands.

"Bow to the judges!" yells the referee.

"Osu!" they grunt, bowing.

"Bow to each other!"

"Osu!" they grunt and bow again.

"Begin!"

The competitors' circle, each looking for an opening to launch an attack.

Many modern derivatives of Combat Jujutsu would declare competition the best way to learn to fight. As the argument goes, "how can you test the techniques of an art unless you are successful with them in competition?"

This argument fails for several reasons. In a prearranged contest, both combatants are usually in good physical condition, both are equally trained and equally armed, usually with the same technical knowledge, and both have come prepared for resistance.

The end result is never death, (although severe injury can and often does happen). There is usually a medic and referee, standing by to keep the competitors safe from serious harm. Let's not forget the corner man who throws in the towel when he feels his fighter has had enough.

In effect they are not testing the technique; rather you are testing the competitor. Therefore, tournaments are not a part of Miyama Ryu Combat Jujutsu.

When we are attacked on the street, there will be no referee, no time for preparatory stances and no formal tournament etiquette. Win or die is often the terms of a serious altercation.

A win will be decided not by a collection of points or even by a knock out, but rather by if you survive the encounter. Your strategy could range from running away, controlling the adversary or even killing him if necessary using any means necessary.

There are no sporting aspects to Miyama Ryu Combat Jujutsu. Many prominent instructors use Jujutsu competitions as a means of reviving the art and to refine their students under adverse conditions. While this strategy has merit, it unfortunately promotes flashy, spectacular techniques that have little real combat value. Or it even dramatically changes the condition of combat so much that it no longer resembles self-defense. For example, a wrestling match that lasts fifteen minutes with both competitors trying to gain an advantage.

Using a sport to test techniques has limited use. As soon as rules are enacted, the nature of the encounter changes.

However, Randori (sparring) is a very important training tool, but to avoid serious injuries even this must be limited in terms of contact and technique.

Using aggressive training drills like the ones described in this book, combined with Randori, will cause the students to compete with the toughest adversary, themselves. Jujutsu is a very personal thing.

Hanging a medal on the wall is not the real goal. The goal is to effectively survive an encounter. The reward is preserving life, yours or the person you are trying to protect.

Taiso (Body Conditioning)

"I work part time teaching computers at an institute that gives 16 – 19 year olds, who the regular school system has failed, a second chance. Most of these boys were expelled from their regular schools for fighting. I came in one day, and immediately noticed the pandemonium.

The staff was rushing about and there was a lot of shouting going on. As it turns out one of the boys was trying to kill another one by striking him over the head with a fire extinguisher. I rushed in and disarmed the boy using a simple wristlock.

He was enraged and had the strength of a madman. (Later I learned that the other boy had bent a metal pipe over his head). He attempted to get around me and attack the other boy.

I continued to control him and forced him into another room and closed the door to isolate him. Then I used an arm lock to bring him to the ground, where I held him for 20 minutes in a ground control until I could get him to calm down."

— Dai-Shihan D'Arcy Rahming

Athletic prowess is not a requirement for practicing effective Combat Jujutsu. The techniques assume that you are weaker than your adversary, outnumbered and didn't have time to warm up.

However, the better your cardiovascular and physical condition, the easier it is to learn and practice the techniques.

Warming up the body, then stretching before class is essential. Not only does this put you in better physical condition, it mentally prepares your body for trauma. Unnecessary injuries such as hamstring pulls are avoided.

The warm-up also builds group spirit, as the counting of repetitions in unison enables the weaker members of the class to be carried by the enthusiasm of the stronger members. During the exercises, everybody in class is equal, regardless of rank or time-in-grade.

Each instructor will have a routine geared towards warm-ups. The following pages illustrate several stretching methods and are intended as a guide only. There are a few methods of toughening the body that are specific to Jujutsu practice. These include toughening the hands for striking and toughening the body for break falls.

Knuckle push-ups on a hardwood floor are an excellent starting point for conditioning the hands for striking. Striking practice should involve the use of hand-held pads. This allows the student to strike full force without risk of injury to his partners. It also allows a safe way of conditioning the student's hands. Additional training tools are heavy bags or Makiwaras (striking posts).

The student should gradually increase his hitting power over a period of years. Training is a lifetime endeavor, so be patient if you try to condition your hands too quickly, there is a possibility of structural damage.

Practicing the actual break falls is the best method of toughening the body for falling. The break falling methods are described in detail in the Ukemi section.

Supplement your training with some kind of aerobic activity, for example cycling or running. When you are first learning techniques of Jujutsu, the pace must be slow and therefore anaerobic. At advanced levels the pace quickens, and your supplemental cardiovascular training proves its worth.

Taiso

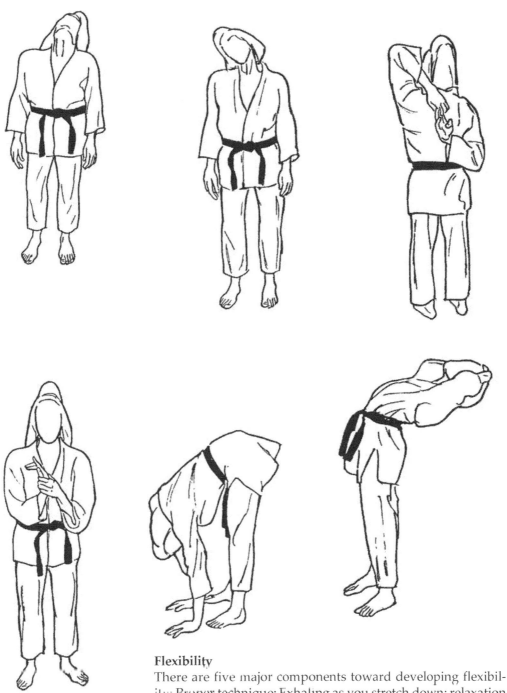

Flexibility
There are five major components toward developing flexibility: Proper technique; Exhaling as you stretch down; relaxation in the stretch; holding the stretch for at least a few seconds; and focusing on the area that you are stretching. Each stretch should be repeated three to five times.

Kamae (Posture and Attitude)

"I have literally taught thousands of people Miyama Ryu Combat Jujutsu. There is no better close quarter combat system out there for law enforcement professionals. Through teaching primarily US Army Rangers, police officers, state troopers, federal agents, and prison STAR Team members over the years I have gotten resounding feedback on the incredible effectiveness of this system. It is a simple system to learn quickly, that delivers results and that you can use now!

At present I am stationed in Iraq and teaching US Soldiers Miyama Ryu Combat Jujutsu everyday. Because these concepts were originally born and tested in war, it was a seamless transition for what US forces need for close quarter protection while conducting the cordon and knock missions that they do everyday. Miyama Ryu is once again being tested in war and has already saved one soldiers life! Through the invaluable concepts of Miyama Ryu Combat Jujutsu many more soldiers will be returning home after completing this mission including yours truly."

— Sensei Daniel M. Wagner, Baghdad, Iraq

Kamae consists of two components – your mental state and physical posture. Many physical confrontations can be avoided entirely by how your adversary reads you. It is not uncommon for victims to be selected on the perception that they are not aware. Miyama Ryu Heiho teaches posture from the very beginning by making you return to a natural state even between the Taisabaki movements.

During an actual confrontation you must be prepared to move from one Kamae to another. Your everyday Kamae is the best starting Kamae for fighting. It gives nothing away. If I clench my fist and drop into a martial arts pose, I have lost any possible element of surprise.

Additionally, I have indicated that I want to fight, because the adversary will interpret a preparatory Kamae in only one way. If the fight does occur, your adversary will be more cautious in his initial attack. He may now choose to use a weapon rather than an empty fist. Witnesses may conclude that you were a trained martial artist and sought the fight. This might create a legal dilemma later on.

Most of the defenses of Combat Jujutsu assume that you do not have time for preparatory Kamae. The Samurai's every action was governed by the thought that he could be attacked at any moment. The ways he sat, ate, walked and even slept were all determined by this possibility. Although it would be extreme to take that approach in every aspect of modern life, in many circumstances, it would be totally appropriate. Jujutsu techniques must never be far from your mind.

Do not turn Jujutsu into just another activity that you practice a few times a week. Never put yourself into a situation in which it would be impossible for you to use your techniques should the need arise.

The strength of many of your techniques comes from a strong foundation. Miyama Ryu uses a few basic Kamae at the beginner level. Incorporate them into your techniques.

The Kamae may not be implemented exactly as you practice them formally; for example, sometimes your center of balance may be higher. But they must be present in some identifiable format, or you will lack balance and the attitude necessary to survive a violent encounter.

Kiai Jutsu (The Spirit Shout)

"It was about midday and I left the supermarket with my hands full of two bags of groceries. I heard footsteps coming up behind me as I made my way to my car. I turned and was surprised to see a man reaching for me. He grabbed me by my shoulders and I immediately yelled" No!" at the top of my lungs, with all my being. He became startled and a look of terror came across his face. He released me and ran off."

— Lisa Wolfe, Minnesota, USA

Kiaijutsu is the art of the spirit shout. Historically, this art was considered to involve centralizing energies in your body and channeling these energies through the use of your voice. Many believe that the ancient masters could bring down a bird in flight with one shout. Some ancient Ryu (schools) claim to have been able to stop a man's heart, or freeze him in place, with a bone-chilling shout. The modern art of Kiai-jutsu is less mystical, but the premise is the same. You can better protect yourself if you understand how to use a spirit shout.

Combat Jujutsu's definition of the spirit shout is that you focus all your intentions into your counterattack. Literally you use your voice as a weapon to intimidate, and defeat the attacker mentally. We all subconsciously practice Kiai. Even a street attacker, who has probably had years of practice in mugging, but no formal martial arts training, knows how to intimidate through the use of his voice and body language. By cursing at his victim and telling him not to resist, the street attacker is effectively trying to crush his victim's will to fight back.

This action is simulated in Combat arts schools to make the training more realistic. When working with a partner, have the partner yell loudly as he attacks. The use of curse words are not necessary, as the point here is that the attacker must try to intimidate and startle the defender. If you train in this manner the shock of a verbal onslaught will be diminished. The street attacker's words will not shake your confidence. And by having a clear mind you can more effectively launch your counter-attack.

To practice terrifying and confusing your adversary with Kiai, you must adopt the mindset of the lion who leaps upon his startled prey. Not only do you want to create confusion for the attacker, but you also want to physically off-balance him, so you can close the distance and defend yourself.

If you are fighting multiple attackers you can sometimes win psychologically by completely terrifying the others with your Kiai and your counter-attack. If you create the perception that you are a violent "Karate Killer," no attacker will want to put his life on the line unless he actually has to. Attackers are generally looking for an easy target, and if they see you are capable of defending yourself, they'll back off.

In some cases Kiai is actually used to educate the attacker. For example, a police officer captures a criminal who is resisting and puts him in a painful wristlock. The criminal wants to comply because of the intense pain, but is so confused that he may injure himself or the officer as he tries to get away from the pain. The police officer gives direction with his voice, "Lay face down! Lay face down!" The attacker complies and the officer cuffs him then releases the painful lock.

Another example of Kiai is if an attacker grabs a would-be victim by the wrists. She strikes him in the kneecap and yells, "No! Let go of me!" The attacker, feeling the pain in his knee, and hearing the forceful command, releases her immediately, giving her time to escape. This worked for Lisa without even using any strikes at all.

Kiai allows you to focus your power. In class develop the attitude of Kiaiing through your entire counter-attack. Your technique ends when your Kiai ends, so consequently, the faster your Kiai, the quicker your execution. By synchronizing your technique, Kiai allows you to control your breathing, so you will not tire as quickly. As you yell, exhale and push your abdomen out. So even if you suffer a blow, your determination will be so intense that your counter-attack will still be successful.

Owaza - The Complete Technique

"I was observing the exhibition of fashion held by Alexander's Department Store, through the window. Suddenly, I felt as if my purse had accidentally opened. When I turned to close it, I noticed that a man, who was standing almost directly behind me, had his hand in my purse.

He was a man in his early thirties, and he seemed to be in an ill state. As soon as I realized what he was doing I pushed him off balance with my right hand. I dropped everything I had with me to the ground and prepared to defend myself. The man suddenly seemed to be very angry and came rushing at me with his right hand open to slap my face.

I blocked against his right arm and gave him an Ippon Seionage. I held him down with my right knee against his armpit and had my left arm holding firmly his right. As I held him in this position, I repeatedly gave him Seiken to the side of his mouth. I kept him in this position until a policeman came to my aid."

—Jennie Rodriguez, New York, USA

Combat Jujutsu's modern derivatives are often confused with actual self-defense methods. In some styles, students are taught that with one miraculous blow they will be able to defeat any adversary. But if one blow could easily kill, why do contact sports and professional boxing have so many survivors? In other styles, a student is taught that once the adversary has been thrown to the ground the fight is over. Unfortunately, both of these assumptions are rarely correct. To assume that you will be able to defeat a large, determined adversary without immobilizing him is foolhardy.

Combat Jujutsu teachers developed the concept of the Owaza so that the counterattack would leave the adversary physically unable to continue the fight. While at times this may appear to be excessive, keep in mind that if your adversary regains his feet, he will be wiser and better prepared. Miyama Ryu Heiho incorporates the Owaza at the physical preparedness level. The Owaza depends on a realistic attack at which point a realistic response is delivered.

An Owaza consists of five techniques:

• The first and most important being the block or evasion.
• The second is some form of misdirection, usually a strike in conjunction with securing the adversary so that he does not escape.
• The third technique is a takedown or major throw.
• The fourth is a strike to further stun the adversary on the ground.
• The fifth is some form of ground control to immobilize the attacker.

All the combat techniques in this book include the concept of the Owaza. However, it is not always necessary or appropriate to apply every element of the Owaza. In each technique, different parts of the Owaza will be explained.

Ukemi (Break Falls)

"Having practiced with a couple of his (Pereira's) students, I'd characterize the Miyama Ryu technique I've seen as quick, brutal, and effective with a high quotient of "f— you" factor. Although Pereira Sensei did study with the Founder of Aikido, his experience in the Bronx has led him to a sharper, more self-defense oriented approach. I would recommend developing strong Ukemi skills (both Judo and Aikido style Ukemi) very quickly if you value your structural integrity. Absolutely do not feed your partner an attack if you're not prepared to deal with a response at the same level of speed and power. (That's good basic advice anyway, but critical advice in this instance)."

— *Comment from the Internet*

Break falls help you conquer the initial fear of practicing the Combat Jujutsu techniques. The forward roll is one of the first techniques taught in the Miyama Ryu. The student soon realizes that he can go head over heels and return to a standing position uninjured. As you advance, leaps over chairs and other obstacles are also practiced.

Ideally, the falling techniques should be practiced on one or two inch mats. The underlying floor should be resilient. Even better is a raised floor with rubber padding underneath. I recommend that each Dojo have a crash pad; a pad that is 3-5 inches thick that is used for learning very difficult falls. The art itself is already very demanding, and the student should not have to worry about injury from a hard surface. If you are going to make an investment in Miyama Ryu, invest in some good mats. Falling is unavoidable to those wishing to learn the full curriculum.

When Shinan Pereira was practicing Aikido in Japan, he received many compliments on his Ukemi. The Shinan spent a lot of time learning the correct falling methods when he first opened his dojo, rather than sacrifice the integrity of the techniques with sloppy Ukemi. He was the Uke for everybody until the students were well versed in Ukemi. There is a practical reason behind this.

The big looping free falls may appear to the uninitiated as just an over dramatization of the effect of a joint manipulation on an individual. The true purpose of the big falls is to allow the defender to practice the technique at full speed and power without risk of injury to the attacker. This is possible because the attacker has twisted his body or joint in the direction of the overextension, thus neutralizing the damaging impact.

Watching a class, it is possible to tell the more adept practitioners by the way they fall. How? A student who is not afraid to take the proper falls will generally have spent more time throwing and being thrown.

Falling involves inescapable discomfort. But if the practitioners concentrate on exhaling as they are thrown, falling will quickly become the easiest part of the workout.

Always practice new methods of falling in the following order. First, falls are practiced from a sitting position, then from a squatting position and finally from a standing position. Get used to slapping the mats with your hands vigorously. The purpose of the slap is twofold: it absorbs some of the force and it aligns the body. Exhale as you hit the ground to avoid having the wind knocked out of you.

Several falling methods are highlighted in this series of books. If you plan to practice Jujutsu as an art, break falls may be your most important asset.

Taisabaki (Body Positioning)

Combat Ju-jutsu utilizes circular motions extensively in meeting an attack. Assuming the attacker is stronger, a weaker defender will always lose if he directly opposes the force. The circular motion allows the Ju-jutsu practitioner to redirect the attacker's force and use it against him. Linear attacks are also utilized, as sometimes it is advantageous to meet an attack head-on.

Taisabaki theory combines circular and linear body positioning. *Taisabaki* involves the defender moving his body out of harm's way and creating an opening for retaliation. Body positioning is an essential element in the art. *Taisabaki* was designed to encompass any attack from any angle. In its most basic form it consists of ten movements against punching attacks. In more advanced forms, it encompasses defenses against armed attacks and multiple assailants.

Taisabaki is an ideal training tool, because one technique can be practiced from ten possible angles. Weapons training, throwing and striking forms are easily incorporated into the *Taisabaki sets.* Experiment with every major technique that you learn, putting it in a *Taisabaki* set.

As you practice the *Taisabaki,* pay special attention to foot placement and the hip rotation.

Proper breathing goes hand in hand with the body positioning. Inhale on the initial evasion or block, then exhale sharply throughout the attack and major technique. The ten basic *Taisabaki* positions are easy to learn and follow a distinct pattern. The pattern is simple if the defender thinks in terms of positioning his body first to the right side and then to the left side.

Taisabaki is the heart of the art; technical skill in striking or major techniques is secondary. If you fail to avoid the initial attack, there is little need for countermoves.

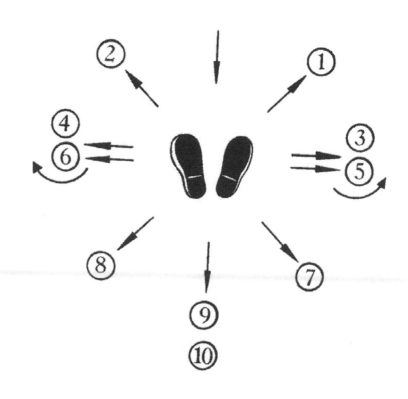

Atemi Waza (Striking Techniques)

Striking and kicking techniques are the first line of defense. In the Miyama Ryu mindset, there are no blocks. Each block is actually an attack against the adversary's attack. Thus the first part of a major technique is usually an attack (block), followed by another attack in the form of a misdirection.

This misdirection unbalances the adversary. In order to successfully apply a major technique such as a joint dislocation or throw, the adversary must first be unbalanced mentally and physically. Physical unbalancing could consist of a penetrating punch, an aggressive pull or even the flinging of a cup of hot coffee.

Any unbalancing must be accompanied by a loud, blood curdling shout. Tighten your abdomen as you shout; this will harden your body. The psychological impact of the yell, compunded with the physical pain of the applied technique, will put the adversary on the defensive. Any accomplices are also frightened, because they now believe you to be a "Karate Killer." Here popular stereotypes can work to your advantage.

Do not forget the concept of the Owaza. It is possible but not probable that the adversary will be defeated solely through striking and kicking methods. Success becomes more improbable when you face multiple attackers. You must always be prepared for a multiple attack, and always be aware that multiple strikes are not efficient. Do not try to turn the fight into a sparring or wrestling match. Never assume you will defeat your adversary with one blow, even though you must strike as though each blow is the only one that matters.

Beginning students generally believe Jujutsu to be a defensive, reactive art. This is a great misconception. Miyama Ryu techniques are proactive. Morally, legally and technically it is best to let the adversary initiate the attack. An attacking adversary must leave some opening for a counterattack. Creating your own openings by initiating an attack is a more advanced concept that will be addressed in later training.

Kote Waza (Wrist Techniques)

"I am a retired Senior Special Agent with the U. S. Treasury Department, Criminal Division. During my tenure I was a national Defensive Tactics Coordinator. I developed, wrote and implemented the Defensive Tactics program for Special Agents and trained over 200 instructor trainers at the Federal Law Enforcement Training Center in Glynco, Georgia. The training program became mandatory for all agents in the department and in currently being taught to new recruits and field agents. The training is all based on Miyama Ryu techniques and tactics."

—*Sensei Don Koz, Illinois, USA*

Kotegaeshi is a major punishment technique. It is effective regardless of the defender's or the attacker's size. It is an excellent tool for redirecting weapons or disarming adversaries. In the classical schools Kotegaeshi played an important role against an armored adversary. Wrist turning attacked one of the Samurai's exposed areas. The Kotegaeshi was employed in conjunction with a short sword, resulting in a fatal conclusion. In modern times the Kotegaeshi still plays a major role, with a different final outcome.

Pressure is applied to the attacker's wrist by the defender crossing his thumbs on the back of the attacker's hand. The wrist is pushed towards the attacker's biceps, then the hand is turned 180 degrees towards the thumb. The wrist turning leaves the attacker on the ground with a dislocated wrist. The initial misdirection and speed of the technique are critical. The technique can be blocked if an adversary is aware that it is being applied and no loosening up has been employed.

Practice the Kotegaeshi keeping your weight low by bending at the knees. The adversary's wrist must be at waist level to enable the defender to use his whole weight against the wrist.

Wrist turning is practiced initially from a formal position at one-quarter speed and power. In advanced drills, wrist turning is practiced at full speed with bone-shattering force. Only practice this way if the Uke is experienced at the free falls, or serious injuries will occur. Give the Uke a chance to take the fall.

Kotegaeshi is the first Kotewaza that is learned in the curriculum. At the Brown Belt divisions, other techniques of wrist turning are practiced. The same care and precision must be taken when practicing these additional techniques. Remember, in the Dojo, injury is our only enemy, so practice these very effective techniques slowly and carefully.

Kansetsu Waza (Joint Techniques)

"Although we use the classical techniques our applications are from the Western perspective. When you throw your arm at me, I'm going to break it if I can. I won't go into histrionics or wasted movements.... I'm going to try to pull that arm out of the socket and shove it down your throat. That's the gist of my defenses."

—*Shinan Antonio Pereira*

Joint locking techniques are formidable major actions against any form of assault. They are the reverse of Kotegaeshi, in that Kotegaeshi overextends the wrist in its natural direction while Kansetsuwaza hyper-extends the elbow in the direction it was not meant to bend. Joint locking techniques render the adversary physically unable to continue the fight. The pain associated with a dislocated elbow is excruciating, but its effectiveness lies in the fact that the arm is immobilized and swings limply against the body.

The basic joint locking defined in this text concerns itself with inflicting punishment onto the elbow of the adversary. The elbow is dislocated. The theory behind the Kansetsuwaza is that pressure must be exerted at the elbow in the direction of the knife-edge of the hand.

Joint locking is extremely useful in close situations where there is not enough room to execute a throw. Like all actions practiced in Miyama Ryu, it is usually preceded by a strike or another form of misdirection.

Care must be taken when practicing these methods. As soon as the Uke feels the pressure of the lock he should slap the side of his body to signal for his partner to stop applying pressure. Joint locking techniques can never be practiced fully without risk of serious injury to the training partner. Even during advanced drills, control during the break is of the utmost importance. No known falling method will protect the student fully from a maliciously applied joint lock.

At the basic level, Kansetsuwaza is applied with the armpit. As the student advances, he soon learns that Kansetsuwaza can be applied with all parts of the body, including knees, elbows, and the torso. The important point is to dislocate the elbow joint.

Nage Waza (Throwing Techniques)

"I saw a man being attacked with a machete, the victim was doing his best to defend the attack with a bucket. I was on duty, I walked to the back of the aggressor and watched and saw that he was in a blind rage, trying his best to do harm to this other fellow. I got behind him and touched him on his back with the palm of my right hand. Just as I expected, he turned. With my left hand, I caught the wrist with the cutlass and using his forward momentum I used Taisabaki 10. He was flipped onto his back, while I had total control of his weapon. He hit the ground and I heard a loud breath. He was totally winded. I rolled him over and put him in an armbar and walked him to the Police Station."

— *Berkley Neely, Nassau, Bahamas*

Full body throws are a core area utilized by Combat Jujutsu practitioners. Historically, a Samurai warrior would throw his adversary to the ground and then dispatch him with his short sword. In contemporary self-defense, a full body throw is instantly followed by a ground control, bringing the fight to a swift conclusion. Many fights now occur in urban areas where there are cement roads and sidewalks. On impact, the adversary experiences full body shock. This pain, along with the psychological shock of being upended, may end the fight instantly.

The Miyama Ryu formal throwing techniques closely follow the principles utilized by Judo practitioners. Jigaro Kano, the founder of Judo, developed the Judo throwing syllabus by combining various Jujutsu styles. Professor Kano then disregarded techniques that he felt did not apply the principle of "maximum efficient use of power." Because Kodokan Judo has become so sport oriented, many of the techniques utilized are unsuitable for life-threatening encounters. These unsuitable techniques involve going to the ground unnecessarily with the adversary. In real combat this could mean death. The Miyama Ryu utilizes only the most practical Kodokan throws.

Miyama Ryu throws fall into two categories, Judo type and Aiki type. The basic throwing techniques of Miyama Ryu Jujutsu involve a combination of unbalancing (see balance diagram), leverage and correct foot and body placement. These principles are isolated and developed most efficiently in formal mode. Each throw has three components: the off balancing, the entrance and the execution.

The initial formal position requires that the Tori and Uke simultaneously grab each other's lapels and elbows. Therefore a right-sided formal position would require that both partners face each other at arms length. Tori grabs Uke's left lapel with his right hand and Uke's right elbow with his left hand. Uke does likewise.

During formal techniques, as always the Uke plays a critical role. The Uke should relax and employ a "going with" attitude. The moves provide an avenue for the instructor to correct flaws in the student's execution and should be practiced without resistance. Since the formal moves are concerned with demonstrating technical ability, in the throws there is no strike or accompanying shout.

As you become more familiar with the throwing techniques, practice them while moving. This allows you to experiment with different angles of entry. Eventually, a form of Randori (free fighting) can evolve, with each practitioner trying to gain an advantage over the other. Caution must be exercised to avoid serious injuries. If one person gains the advantage, the other should go with the throw. This is a good confidence builder. If you can throw an equally skilled, resisting partner, there should be no doubt in your mind that you can throw an adversary who has been stunned.

One effective practice method is uchikomi, which allows you to practice the off balancing and entrance without the execution. This is a particularly good practice method as you get older and do not feel like being upended all the time.

Shime Waza (Strangulation)

"I was playing a friendly game of neighborhood basketball when it all went wrong. My opponent became enraged after I had beaten him and began to threaten me. I told him to calm down and accept his loses like a man. This enraged him even further and he began to swing on me. I blocked him a couple of times using Taisabaki and backing up, continuously telling him to stop. Feeling frustrated that he could not hit me he yelled that he was going to his car to get his gun. At this point I turned him around into a chokehold. He gave up after a few seconds and I released him and got in my car and left."

— *Willis Lawrence James III, Georgia, USA*

Shime Waza is the art of strangulation. To safely end a violent confrontation, usually with minimum harm to the adversary, Miyama Ryu practitioners heavily utilize it. In Miyama Ryu, chokes take on two forms, trachea and carotid.

Trachea chokes must be practiced with extreme care so that the Tori does not damage the Uke. The idea of trachea chokes in combat is to damage and crush the trachea, thus disabling or even killing the adversary. These must be done only in extreme circumstances.

Carotid chokes are also very effective, keeping in mind that you must control the adversary's body before applying the choke. These cause unconsciousness, but can also kill if you decide to continue to hold the adversary after he has passed out.

There has been a lot of study done on carotid chokes, by the Judo community. These studies have yielded the following conclusions.

1. Carotid chokes cut off oxygen supply to the brain causing unconsciousness typically in 8 – 14 seconds. Typically the unconscious person regains consciousness within 10 – 20 seconds without intervention.

2. In chokes without utilizing clothing, (Hadaka Shime) the pressure on the trachea and larynx can be quite painful, in addition to causing unconsciousness.

3. Convulsions similar to short epileptic seizures can occur.

4. Increased heart rate, increased blood pressure, and dilatation of the pupils can also occur.

5. There are no deleterious after effects to being choked.

Shime Waza is an effective and powerful tool that should not be neglected in training.

Kyusho (Targeting Vital Areas)

"At approximately 2 a.m. on the corner of Morris Ave and 166th street I saw my brother and a friend being beaten up by 7 guys. Not knowing if my brother was in the right or the wrong I ran to his aid. I rid myself of my first opponent by giving him Shuto blows to the neck and kicking him in the back.

My second opponent I overcame by giving him a full shoulder throw and applying the principle of 3. At this time my third opponent was on my back. He received a full hip throw. By this time a crowd was attracted and the remaining attackers attempted to flee."

— *Joseph Rinaldi, New York, USA*

Knowledge of the body's vital areas is essential to Combat Jujutsu, as relevant now as in the day of the Samurai. During battle the Samurai wore light flexible armor. Atemi Waza was rarely used on the battlefield, but found its applications in street defense. In almost all cases, to strike at random against a sword-wielding adversary meant certain death. This led to the motto of many ancient Combat Karate-Jujutsu schools: "One blow, one victory."

Miyama Ryu makes a clear distinction between pressure points and vital areas. Pressure points involve pain compliance techniques and are very specific in their applications.

A police officer might find the use of pressure points appropriate against a passively resisting, unarmed suspect. This same officer, fighting for his life against an armed individual, must choose the right level of force necessary to subdue the aggressor. His defense would undoubtedly involve a strike to a vital area.

The lower grades of Miyama Ryu concentrate on survival of the student. Controls and pain compliance are practiced only after the self-defense foundation has been achieved.

A scientific understanding of vital areas enables you to attack the weakest points of the body. For example, the skull has many sutures, where the bones knit together. To strike at points along these sutures would cause tremendous damage. Knowledge of vital areas must be accompanied by great care and control to assure safe practice.

Where you strike will depend on the adversary's clothing, the local conditions or the nature of the encounter. In today's environment nobody wears armor. Or do they? A heavy winter coat can probably deflect the force of a well-placed blow. It's difficult to strike with precision if you can't identify vital points through heavy clothing. In a dark alley the face is a harder target to hit than a vital area on the body.

Top of the head

Center of forehead

Between nose and
upper lip

Chin

Larynx

Solar plexus

Base of ribs

Elbow

2 inches above
navel

Wrist

Groin

Knee

Instep

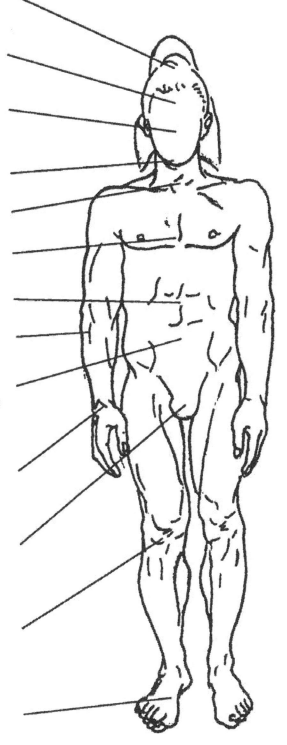

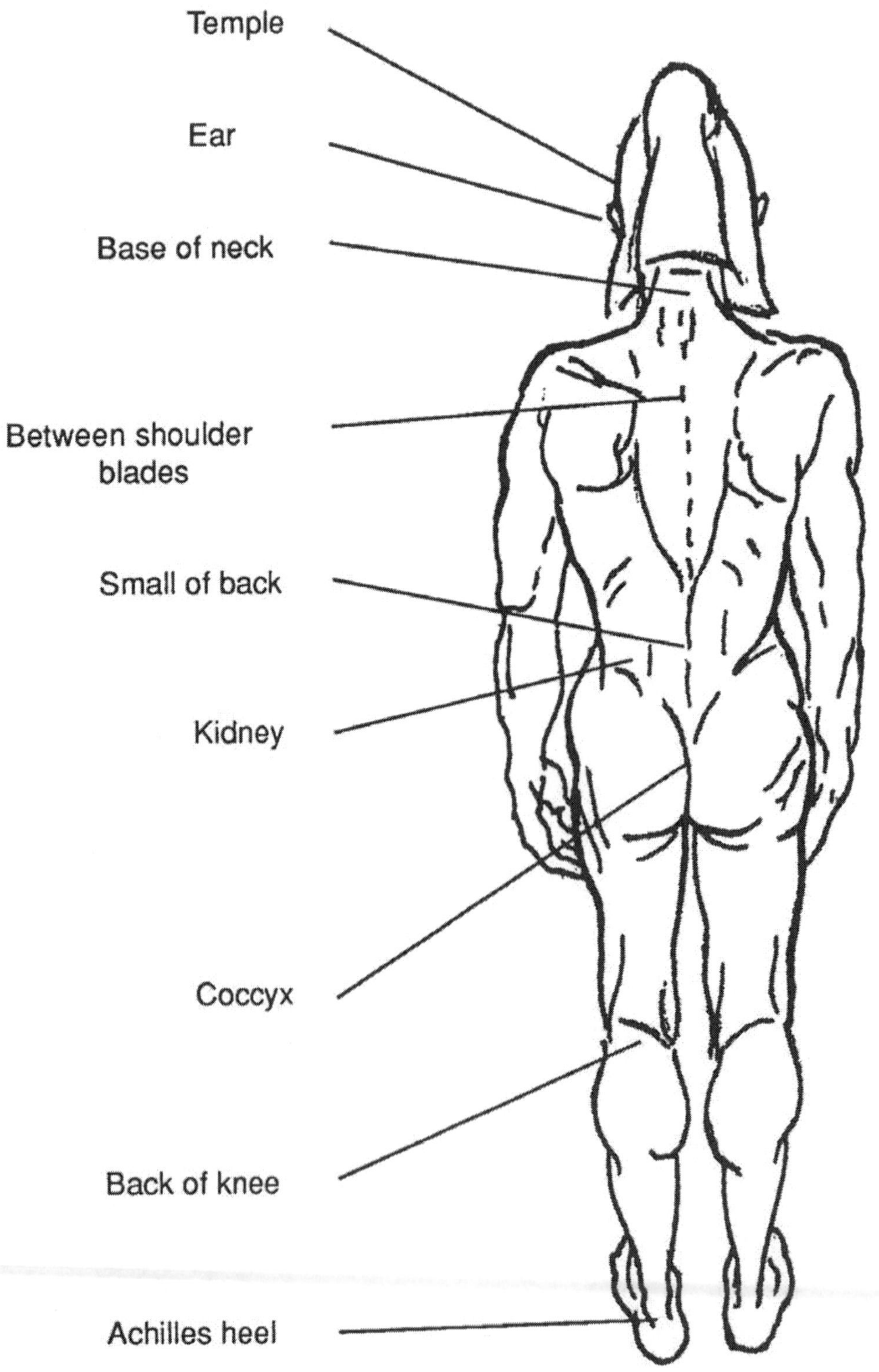

Temple

Ear

Base of neck

Between shoulder
blades

Small of back

Kidney

Coccyx

Back of knee

Achilles heel

Maai (Combative Distance)

"While on patrol I received a report that an armed robber had escaped and had been spotted hiding in a grave yard. My partner and I split up and went among the graves attempting to find the perpetrator.

As I approached a large tombstone I heard some noise behind me. I turned and saw a man with a machete rushing at me. I immediately threw him with an Ippon Seionage and he went over my back and fell on the concrete slab of the grave.

I proceeded to turn him over, (he offered no resistance), and place him in a ground control. It had happened so fast that it was only then that I realized he was unconscious."

— Franklyn Dorsett, Nassau, Bahamas

There are several distances involved in the practice of Miyama Ryu. The first distance is an attack that is effective from more than three steps away. This distance usually involves firearms or other projectile weapons. Though no direct techniques will address these kinds of attacks, the sense of awareness gained from the practice of Combat Jujutsu will enable you to avoid many of these unrecoverable situations.

The second distance is an attack that is effective from two steps away. This attack would involve a club, a baseball bat, or a machete. The vital fact is that now you are in effective fighting range. Many defenses will involve meeting the weapon or avoiding it entirely. If you step in to meet the attack, you must do so quickly.

The third distance is an attack that can be launched from about one step away. This would include empty-handed techniques or short weapons such as knives or black jacks. Almost every self-defense program or modern martial art will address attacks of this nature.

Full body grabs, mugs and other body contact attacks define the fourth distance. Here the attack is effective from arms length. Fighting from the ground also falls into this category. This category has seen a recent surge in interest in the modern arts.

Any effective fighting system will take into account these four distances. The Miyama Ryu concentrates on all four, giving each equal weight in order to prepare the students adequately for the street.

Timing

"I am a U.S. Marine in the reserves. Once on a deployment, I was sitting on a bed in a barrack that we were sharing with another service. I was reading a book when a group of people came into the barrack that had been out drinking.

One of the gentlemen confronted me. He told me that he had heard that I was a martial artist and that he was going to kick my ass. I told him that I was sure that he could and did not make any trouble.

He made some more comments and then walked away. Next thing I knew he was yelling and running at me like a football player. Not thinking I dropped the book that I was reading grabbed him and did a Tomoenage (stomach throw). The timing was perfect. He went over the bed I was sitting on and over the next bed. Then he hit the wall with his back. There was a good amount of momentum.

The roll landed me on my feet. I then sat on the bed between the back wall and him. I then pushed the bed into his stomach and applied pressure until his friends took him away."

— Sensei Zurriane Bennett, Washington D.C., USA

Timing is of the utmost importance in Combat Jujutsu. Speed is a factor, but only to the extent that you have to move just fast enough to avoid the attack. For example, if a train comes at you at one hundred miles an hour it is only necessary to move just before impact - and just far enough so that you are no longer in harm's way. This idea carries over to combat. After you avoid an attack, you do not want to be in a position that puts you too far from your adversary to retaliate.

There are three possible timings to an attack. The first is that you initiate the attack (Sen Sen no Sen). This strategy is necessary if the adversary has not drawn his weapon and you are closing the distance. But any attack must leave you open in some way. There are also moral and legal implications to attacking first.

The second timing is to meet the attack as it occurs (Sen no Sen). This is the level that we aspire to in Miyama Ryu Jujutsu. As the adversary draws back to make the attack you should automatically begin your attack. Miyama Ryu should be thought of as an art of attack and not simply defense.

The third timing is to block, and then counterattack (Go no Sen). Blocking is necessary if we are surprised or his attack is too quick to perform the second timing. If we assume the weapon is already drawn, this timing should be viewed in most cases, as superior to the first but inferior to the second.

The type of timing that you use will depend on your circumstances. The most important thing is to survive the violent encounter.

Promotion Requirements for 6th Kyu Orange Belt

6th Kyu Orange Belt

Question 1 - Formal Bow and Ukemi

Formal Bow

The bow is used in Miyama Ryu as a symbol of respect. It is the equivalent of a handshake. Just as you would not extend someone a limp wrist for a handshake, you should also try to always bow in a courteous manner. Also as someone bows you return the bow simultaneously. Depending on the situation different bows are utilized. For example a standing bow for informal practice is common. During Kata or on special occasions, a kneeling bow from the Seiza position, or what is commonly refered to as the Jujutsu bow is also utilized.

Back fall

Stand in a natural position, hands hang loosely at your side. Raise your hands to shoulder height Squat, bending both knees. Throw yourself backwards. Tuck your chin into your chest to avoid hitting your head on the ground. Tighten your abdomen by exhaling. Slap the ground vigorously. Land on your back exhaling sharply. Keep your chin tucked in. Bring your knees up. If an adversary is standing over you, this provides some protection.

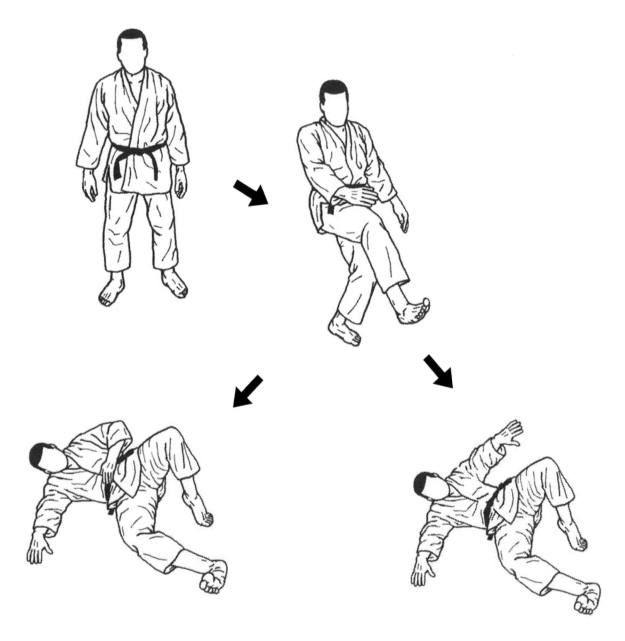

Side fall

Stand in a natural position, hands hang loosely at the side. Bring your right leg forward. Bend your right knee and raise your right hand. Slap the ground. Tighten your abdomen by exhaling sharply. Land on your right side.

This technique can be done with one hand or two hands.

Question 1c - Front Roll

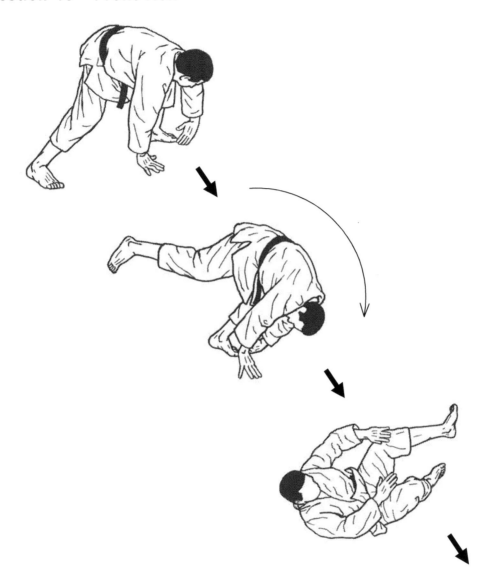

Front roll

Stand with your left foot forward, right hand touching the ground. Your left elbow should point in the direction of your roll. Push off with your feet and roll along your pinkie finger, your arm and diagonally across your back. At no point should your head touch the ground. As you roll tuck the trailing leg in and perform a complete arc with the lead leg. On completion of your roll you should return to the same position that you began with.

Question 2 - Taisabaki Escape and Formal

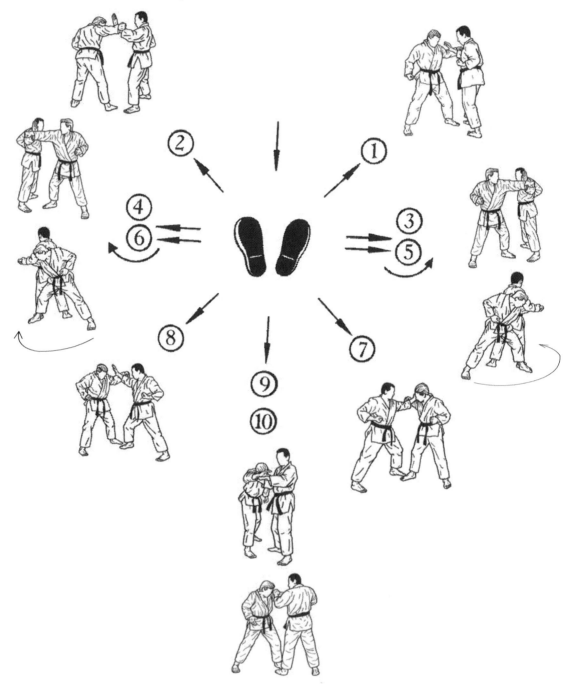

Taisabaki Escape and Formal
This series of steps is first practiced without a partner using a shuffling
step (tsugi ashi) in the ten directions. Then Taisabaki formal is practiced
with a partner with just the escaping body positions and blocking
movements.

Taisabaki 1   Tori
Stand in a relaxed natural position facing adversary. As adversary attacks with a hooking left punch, step forward into a right stance. Inhale sharply. Bring the right arm up and execute a Kote attack to the adversary's lower forearm. Chamber your left hand, making a tight fist. Twist your hips forward. Strike with left Seiken to the adversary's chin. Simultaneously chamber your right arm back. Kiai loudly as you strike.

Taisabaki 1   Uke
Stand in a relaxed natural position facing adversary. Step forward with your left foot. Execute a left hooking punch to the adversary's right cheek. Exhale sharply, yelling as you strike. As the adversary punches, move your head back slightly, simulating that you have been struck.

Taisabaki 2   Tori
Stand in a relaxed natural position facing adversary. As adversary attacks with a hooking right punch, step forward into a left stance. Inhale sharply. Bring the left arm up and execute a Kote attack to the adversary's lower forearm. Chamber your right hand, making a tight fist. Twist your hips forward. Strike with right Seiken to the adversary's chin. Simultaneously chamber your left arm back. Kiai loudly as you strike.

Taisabaki 2   Uke
Stand in a relaxed natural position facing adversary. Step forward with your right foot . Execute a right hooking house punch to the adversary's left cheek. Exhale sharply, yelling as you strike. As the adversary strikes, move your head back slightly, simulating that you have been struck.

6th Kyu Orange Belt

Taisabaki 3   Tori

Stand in a relaxed natural position facing adversary. Step laterally with your right foot. Depending on the distance to the adversary your step may be obliquely toward him. Bring the left arm up and execute a circular block against the attacking left arm. Simultaneously chamber your right hand back. Inhale on the block. Execute a right Seiken strike to the adversary's kidneys. Simultaneously chamber your left hand in preparation for another strike. Kiai as you strike.

Taisabaki 3   Uke

Stand in a relaxed natural position facing adversary. Step forward with your left leg and strike with a left thrust to the adversary's face. Exhale and Kiai as you strike. As the defender counter strikes simulate being struck in the kidney.

Taisabaki 4   Tori

Stand in a relaxed natural position facing adversary. Step laterally with your left foot. Depending on the distance to the adversary your step may be obliquely toward him. Bring the right arm up and execute a Kote against the attacking right arm. Simultaneously chamber your left hand back. Inhale on the block. Execute a left Seiken strike to the adversary's kidneys. Simultaneously chamber your right hand in preparation for another strike. Exhale and Kiai as you strike.

Taisabaki 4   Uke

Stand in a relaxed natural position facing adversary. Step forward with your right leg and strike with a right thrust to the adversary's face. Kiai as you strike. As the defender counter strikes simulate being struck in the kidney.

6th Kyu Orange Belt

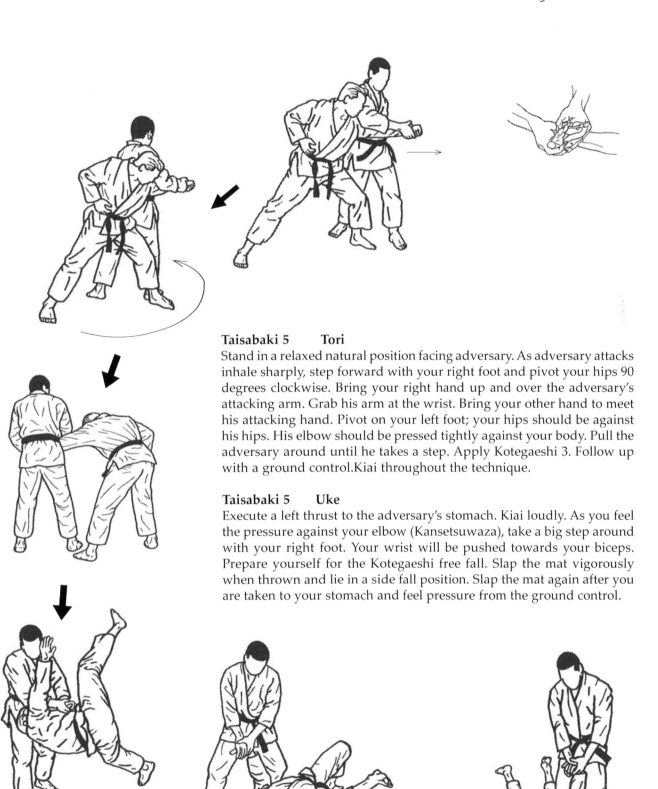

Taisabaki 5   Tori
Stand in a relaxed natural position facing adversary. As adversary attacks inhale sharply, step forward with your right foot and pivot your hips 90 degrees clockwise. Bring your right hand up and over the adversary's attacking arm. Grab his arm at the wrist. Bring your other hand to meet his attacking hand. Pivot on your left foot; your hips should be against his hips. His elbow should be pressed tightly against your body. Pull the adversary around until he takes a step. Apply Kotegaeshi 3. Follow up with a ground control.Kiai throughout the technique.

Taisabaki 5   Uke
Execute a left thrust to the adversary's stomach. Kiai loudly. As you feel the pressure against your elbow (Kansetsuwaza), take a big step around with your right foot. Your wrist will be pushed towards your biceps. Prepare yourself for the Kotegaeshi free fall. Slap the mat vigorously when thrown and lie in a side fall position. Slap the mat again after you are taken to your stomach and feel pressure from the ground control.

Taisabaki 6   Tori
Stand in a relaxed natural position facing adversary. As adversary attacks inhale sharply, step forward with your left foot and pivot your hips 90 degrees clockwise. Bring your left hand up and over the adversary's attacking arm. Grab his arm at the wrist. Bring your other hand to meet his attacking hand. Pivot on your left foot; your hips should be against his hips. His elbow should be pressed tightly against your body. Pull the adversary around until he takes a step. Apply Kotegaeshi 3. Follow up with a ground control. Kiai throughout the technique.

Taisabaki 6   Uke
Execute a right thrust to the adversary's stomach. Kiai loudly. As you feel the pressure against your elbow (Kansetsuwaza), take a big step around with your left foot. Your wrist will be pushed towards your biceps. Prepare yourself for the Kotegaeshi free fall. Slap the mat vigorously when thrown and lie in a side fall position. Slap the mat again after you are taken to your stomach and feel pressure from the ground control.

Taisabaki 7   Tori
Stand in a relaxed natural position facing adversary. As adversary attacks with a wild hooking right punch, step back with your right leg, bending your left knee. Inhale sharply. Bring the left arm up and execute a Kote strike to the adversary's lower forearm. Chamber your right hand, making a tight fist. Twist your hips forward. Strike with right Seiken to the adversary's chin. Simultaneously chamber your left arm back. Kiai loudly as you strike.

Taisabaki 7   Uke
Stand in a relaxed natural position facing adversary. Step forward with your right foot Execute a wild hooking right punch to the adversary's left cheek. Kiai as you strike. As the adversary strikes, move your head back slightly, simulating that you have been struck.

Taisabaki 8   Tori
Stand in a relaxed natural position facing adversary. As adversary attacks with a wild hooking left punch, step back with your left leg bending your right knee. Inhale sharply. Bring the right arm up and execute a Kote strike to the adversary's lower forearm. Chamber your left hand, making a tight fist. Twist your hips forward. Strike with left Seiken to the adversary's chin. Simultaneously chamber your right arm back. Kiai loudly as you strike.

Taisabaki 8   Uke
Stand in a relaxed natural position facing adversary. Step forward with your left foot. Execute a wild hooking punch to the adversary's right cheek. Kiai as you strike. As the adversary strikes, move your head back slightly, simulating that you have been struck.

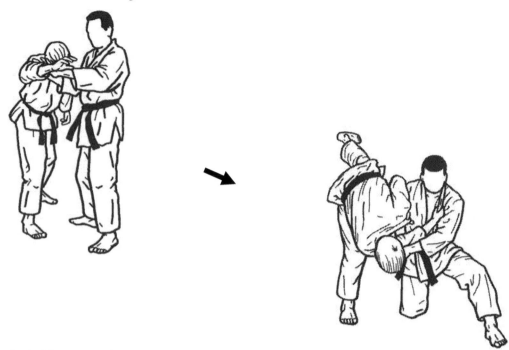

Taisabaki 9   Tori

Stand in a natural position. As adversary pushes, wait until the last possible moment to move. Pivot on your right foot, step back with your left leg. Turn counterclockwise, drop to your right knee, pulling the adversary's arm outward. Continue to pull the adversary's arm between his legs, forming a full circle. Strike Shuto to the bridge of the nose. Use a downward chopping motion. Kiai as you throw.

Taisabaki 9   Uke

Push the defender very aggressively with your right hand to his left shoulder. Kiai loudly. As the defender pulls let your momentum carry you. Raise your left leg in preparation for the free fall. Execute a free fall and slap the ground vigorously. Do not rise immediately or you will be struck accidentally in the jaw.

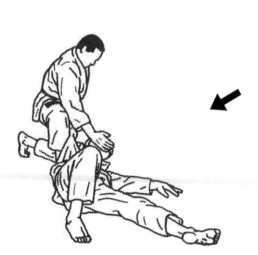

Taisabaki 10   Tori

Stand in a natural position. As adversary pushes, wait until the last possible moment to move. Pivot on your left foot and step back with your right leg. Turn counterclockwise, drop to your left knee, pulling the adversary's arm outward. Continue to pull the adversary's arm between his legs, forming a full circle. Strike Shuto to the bridge of the nose. Use a downward chopping motion. Kiai as you throw.

Taisabaki 10   Uke

Push the defender very aggressively with your left hand to his right shoulder. Kiai loudly. As the defender pulls let your momentum carry you. Raise your right leg in preparation for the free fall. Execute a free fall and slap the ground vigorously. Do not rise immediately or you will be struck accidentally in the jaw.

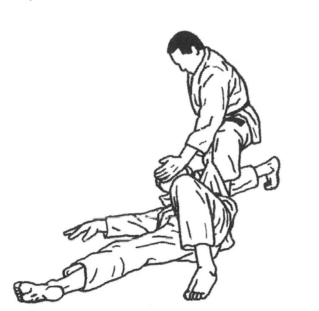

Question 3- Kotegaeshi

Kotegaeshi 1   Tori
Step forward with your left foot. Grab the adversary's right hand with your thumb on the back of his hand, fingers on his palm. Bring the other hand up so that the thumbs cross on the back of the adversary's hand, fingers on his palm. Press his hand towards his bicep. Step diagonally across. Bring your right leg behind the adversary's right leg. Apply pressure to his wrist in the direction of his thumb. The adversary will fall to his back with a broken wrist. There is no audible kiai in the formal movement.

Kotegaeshi 1   Uke
Stand in a relaxed position. Extend your right hand forward slightly. Your balance will be broken to your right rear corner. Resist the wrist twisting action as long as you can until you are so off balanced that you are blocked from stepping forward. Take a free fall over his extended leg. Exhale sharply. Slap the ground vigorously on impact.

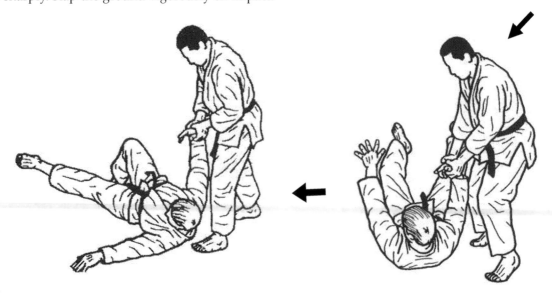

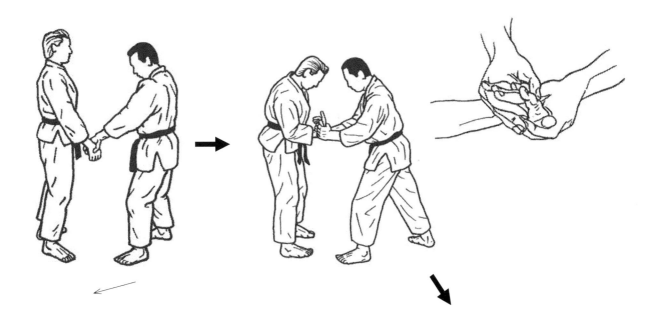

Kotegaeshi 2   Tori

Step forward with your left foot. Grab the adversary's right hand with your thumb on the back of his hand, fingers on his palm. Bring the other hand up so that the thumbs cross on the back of the adversary's hand, fingers on his palm. Press his hand towards his bicep. Keep the adversary's wrist at your waist level. Apply pressure in the direction of his thumb, turning his wrist completely over. Rotate at the waist and use your whole body in applying pressure. The adversary's wrist will break and he will be thrown to the ground. Hold the adversary's wrist for two seconds to show control then step back to a natural position. There is no audible Kiai in the formal movement.

Kotegaeshi 2   Uke

Stand in a relaxed position. Extend your right hand forward slightly. Take a free fall, exhaling sharply. Slap the ground vigorously on impact.

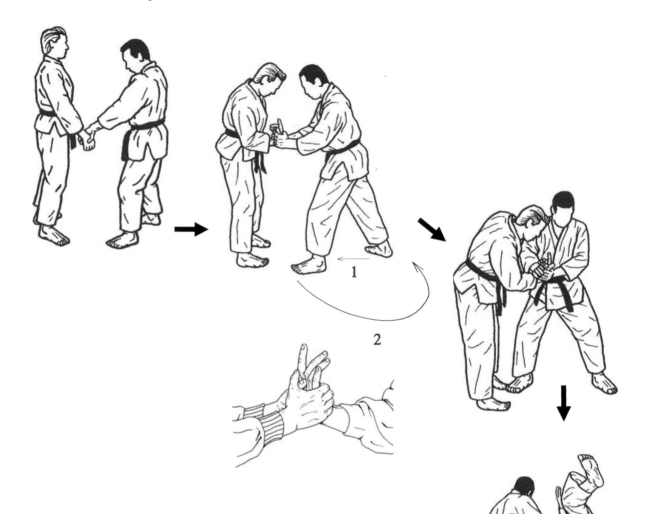

Kotegaeshi 3   Tori
Step forward with your left foot. Grab the adversary's right hand with your thumb on the back of his hand, fingers on his palm. Bring the other hand up so that the thumbs cross on the back of the adversary's hand, fingers on his palm. Press his hand towards the bicep. Keep the adversary's wrist at your waist level. Step in with your right leg. Pivot 90 to 180 degrees on your right foot. Keep his locked wrist in front of you, waist high. Apply pressure in the direction of his thumb, turning his wrist completely over. Rotate at the waist and use your whole body in applying pressure. The adversary's wrist will break and he will be thrown to the ground. Hold the adversary's wrist for two seconds to show control then step back to a natural position. There is no audible Kiai in the formal movement.

Kotegaeshi 3   Uke
Stand in a relaxed position. Extend your right hand forward slightly. Your balance will be broken to your right front corner. Take a free fall, exhaling sharply. Slap the ground vigorously on impact.

6th Kyu Orange Belt

Question 4- Kansetsuwaza

Kansetsuwaza Step In Step Out   Tori

Step in with your right foot diagonally. Grab the adversary's right hand with your right hand. Step back out with your right foot. Bring your left hand to your right with ten fingers together at the wrist. Step in front of the adversary's right foot with your left foot. Bring your left armpit over the adversary's elbow. This action will lock the adversary in. Brace down with your armpit on the adversary's elbow. Simultaneously pull his wrist up in the direction of the knife edge of his hand. Exhale and tighten your abdomen. This action will break the adversary's elbow and drive his head into your knee. Bring the adversary down strongly by stepping your left leg across your right, maintaining pressure on the dislocated elbow. Immobilize the adversary by trapping his elbow between your knees. Apply pressure, pushing his arm diagonally across his head. This action will dislocate the shoulder if done in an abrupt manner. There is no audible Kiai in the formal movement.

Kansetsuwaza Step In Step Out   Uke

Stand in a natural position, right hand slightly forward. Do not step but allow your balance to be broken forward. As your elbow is locked, bend forward slightly. Slap the side of your body as you feel pressure on your elbow. You will be fully unbalanced at this point and unable to step. Fall forward, turning your head away from the captured arm. This will alleviate the pressure. Slap the mat vigorously when you feel pressure on your shoulder.

Double Wrist Grab Kansetsuwaza   Tori

Stand in a relaxed natural position. The adversary will grab both of your wrists. Grab his right wrist with your left hand. Your fingers should be up. Strike with left Mae Geri to the adversary's knee. Step in left foot and apply Kansetsuwaza to the adversary's elbow. Bring him to the ground strongly and immobilize him with your ground control. Kiai throughout the technique.

Double Wrist Grab Kansetsuwaza   Uke

Grab both of the defender's wrists and Kiai. Direct your attention to your knee after being kicked. As your elbow is locked, bend forward slightly. Slap the side of your body as you feel pressure on your elbow. You will be fully unbalanced at this point and unable to step. Fall forward, turning your head away from the captured arm. This will alleviate the pressure. Slap the mat vigorously when you feel pressure on your shoulder.

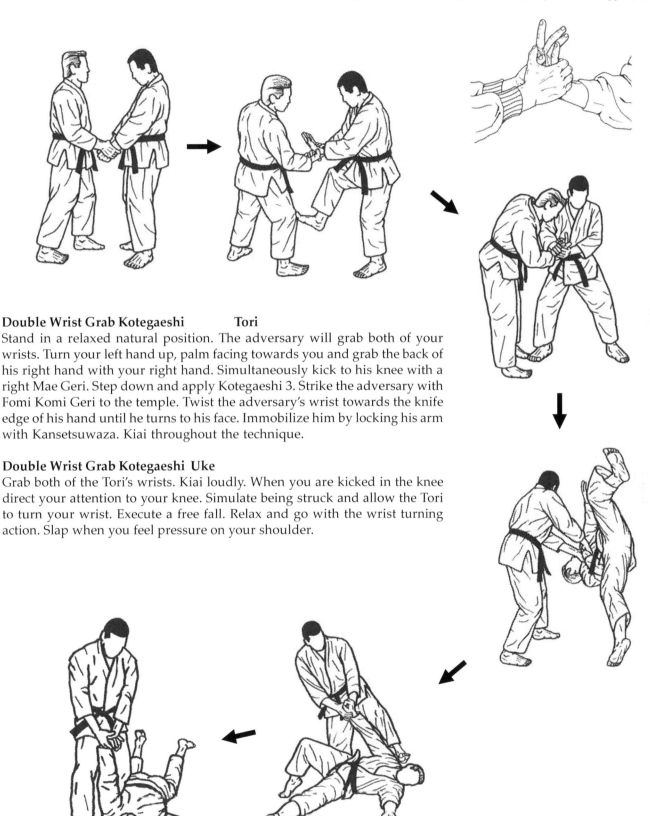

Double Wrist Grab Kotegaeshi   Tori
Stand in a relaxed natural position. The adversary will grab both of your wrists. Turn your left hand up, palm facing towards you and grab the back of his right hand with your right hand. Simultaneously kick to his knee with a right Mae Geri. Step down and apply Kotegaeshi 3. Strike the adversary with Fomi Komi Geri to the temple. Twist the adversary's wrist towards the knife edge of his hand until he turns to his face. Immobilize him by locking his arm with Kansetsuwaza. Kiai throughout the technique.

Double Wrist Grab Kotegaeshi Uke
Grab both of the Tori's wrists. Kiai loudly. When you are kicked in the knee direct your attention to your knee. Simulate being struck and allow the Tori to turn your wrist. Execute a free fall. Relax and go with the wrist turning action. Slap when you feel pressure on your shoulder.

Single Wrist Grab Kansetsuwaza   Tori
Stand in a relaxed natural position. The adversary will grab your left wrist with his right hand. Grab his right wrist with your left hand. Your fingers should be up. Strike Seiken to a vital point on the adversary's face. Step in left foot and apply Kansetsuwaza to the adversary's elbow. Bring him to the ground strongly and immobilize him with your ground control. Kiai throughout the technique.

Single Wrist Grab Kansetsuwaza   Uke
Grab the defender's left wrist aggressively with your right hand. Kiai loudly. Move your head back to simulate being struck. As your elbow is locked, bend forward slightly. Slap the side of your body as you feel pressure on your elbow. You will be fully unbalanced at this point and unable to step. Fall forward turning your head away from the captured arm. This will alleviate the pressure. Slap the mat vigorously when you feel pressure on your shoulder.

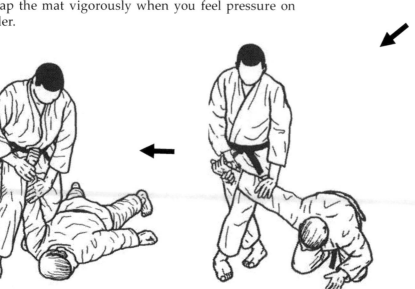

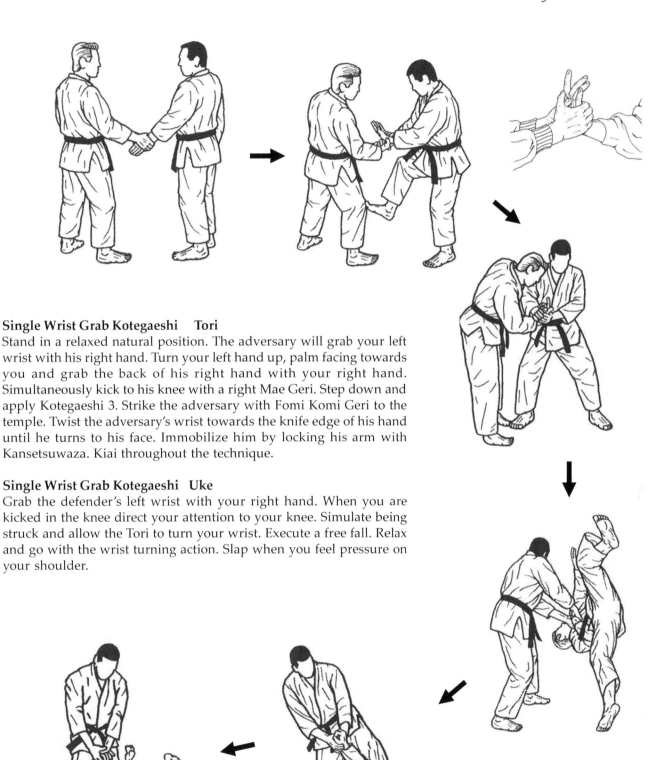

Single Wrist Grab Kotegaeshi   Tori
Stand in a relaxed natural position. The adversary will grab your left wrist with his right hand. Turn your left hand up, palm facing towards you and grab the back of his right hand with your right hand. Simultaneously kick to his knee with a right Mae Geri. Step down and apply Kotegaeshi 3. Strike the adversary with Fomi Komi Geri to the temple. Twist the adversary's wrist towards the knife edge of his hand until he turns to his face. Immobilize him by locking his arm with Kansetsuwaza. Kiai throughout the technique.

Single Wrist Grab Kotegaeshi   Uke
Grab the defender's left wrist with your right hand. When you are kicked in the knee direct your attention to your knee. Simulate being struck and allow the Tori to turn your wrist. Execute a free fall. Relax and go with the wrist turning action. Slap when you feel pressure on your shoulder.

Question - Lapel Grabs

Double Lapel Grab Kansetsuwaza   Tori
Stand in a relaxed natural position. The adversary will grab you by both lapels. The knife edge of his hands must be facing downwards or it will be too difficult to untangle him. Grab his right wrist with your left hand to secure him. Strike Seiken to a vital area in his face. Step forward with your left foot and apply Kansetsuwaza to the adversary's elbow. Bring him to the ground strongly and immobilize him with your ground control. Kiai throughout the technique.

Double Lapel Grab Kansetsuwaza   Uke
Grab the defender's lapels aggressively with both hands. Move your head back to simulate being struck. As your elbow is locked, bend forward slightly. Slap the side of your body as you feel pressure on your elbow. You will be fully unbalanced at this point and unable to step. Fall forward, turning your head away from the captured arm. This will alleviate the pressure. Slap the mat vigorously when you feel pressure on your shoulder.

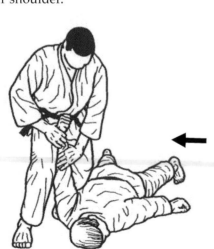

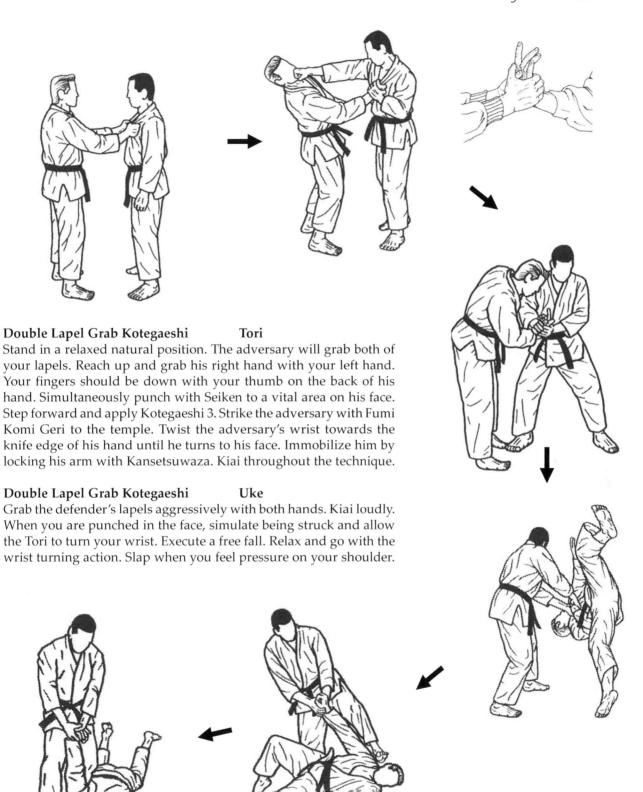

Double Lapel Grab Kotegaeshi   Tori
Stand in a relaxed natural position. The adversary will grab both of
your lapels. Reach up and grab his right hand with your left hand.
Your fingers should be down with your thumb on the back of his
hand. Simultaneously punch with Seiken to a vital area on his face.
Step forward and apply Kotegaeshi 3. Strike the adversary with Fumi
Komi Geri to the temple. Twist the adversary's wrist towards the
knife edge of his hand until he turns to his face. Immobilize him by
locking his arm with Kansetsuwaza. Kiai throughout the technique.

Double Lapel Grab Kotegaeshi   Uke
Grab the defender's lapels aggressively with both hands. Kiai loudly.
When you are punched in the face, simulate being struck and allow
the Tori to turn your wrist. Execute a free fall. Relax and go with the
wrist turning action. Slap when you feel pressure on your shoulder.

Single Lapel Grab Kansetsuwaza   Tori
Stand in a relaxed natural position. The adversary will grab you by your lapel. The knife edge of his hand must be facing downwards or it will be too difficult to untangle him. Grab his right wrist with your left hand to secure him. Strike Seiken to a vital area in his face. Step forward with your left foot and apply Kansetsuwaza to the adversary's elbow. Bring him to the ground strongly and immobilize him with your ground control. Kiai throughout the technique.

Single Lapel Grab Kansetsuwaza   Uke
Grab the defender's lapel aggressively with your right hand. Move your head back to simulate being struck. As your elbow is locked, bend forward slightly. Slap the side of your body as you feel pressure on your elbow. You will be fully unbalanced at this point and unable to step. Fall forward, turning your head away from the captured arm. This will alleviate the pressure. Slap the mat vigorously when you feel pressure on your shoulder.

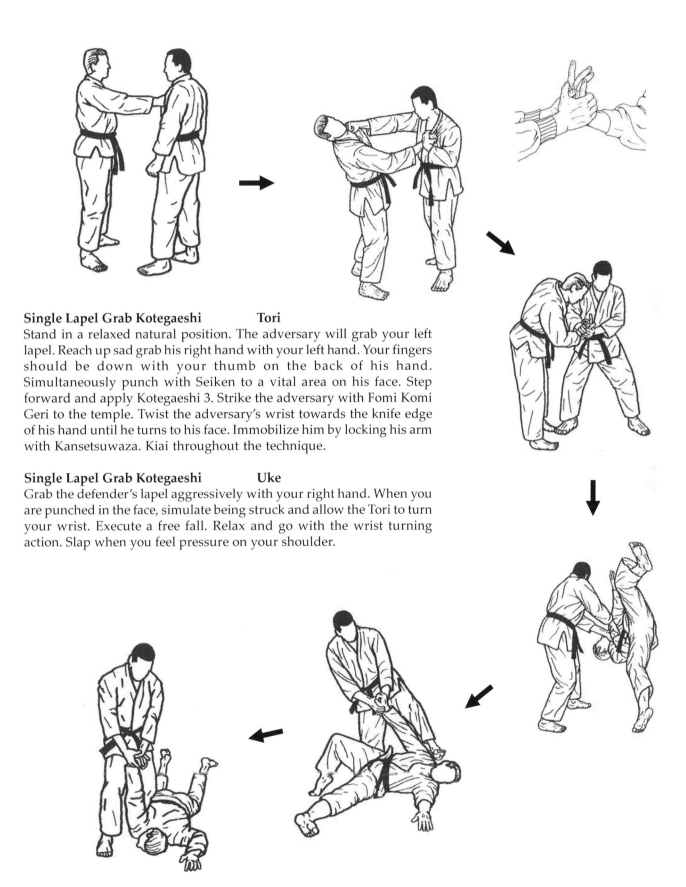

Single Lapel Grab Kotegaeshi   Tori

Stand in a relaxed natural position. The adversary will grab your left lapel. Reach up sad grab his right hand with your left hand. Your fingers should be down with your thumb on the back of his hand. Simultaneously punch with Seiken to a vital area on his face. Step forward and apply Kotegaeshi 3. Strike the adversary with Fomi Komi Geri to the temple. Twist the adversary's wrist towards the knife edge of his hand until he turns to his face. Immobilize him by locking his arm with Kansetsuwaza. Kiai throughout the technique.

Single Lapel Grab Kotegaeshi   Uke

Grab the defender's lapel aggressively with your right hand. When you are punched in the face, simulate being struck and allow the Tori to turn your wrist. Execute a free fall. Relax and go with the wrist turning action. Slap when you feel pressure on your shoulder.

Question 7 - Rear Upper Chest Grab

Rear upper arms   Tori

Stand in a natural position. The adversary will seize you aggressively around your chest with both arms above your elbows. Bend at the knees and raise both arms. This will lower your weight and allow you to escape the grab. Throw the adversary on to his side with Ippon Seionage. Strike Fomi Komi Geri to his temple and immediately look for another aggressor. Kiai throughout the technique.

Rear upper arms   Uke

Grab the defender around the chest with both arms. There must be no space between your bodies. Take a side fall over the defender's back. Exhale as you hit the ground. Slap the mat vigorously.

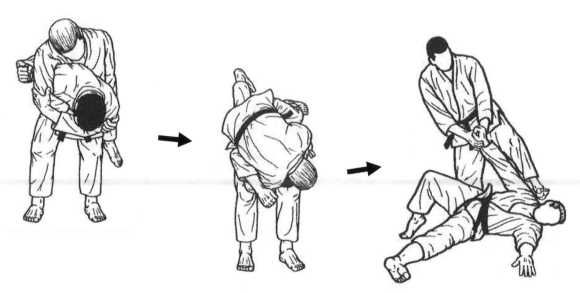

6th Kyu Orange Belt

Question 8 - Mugs

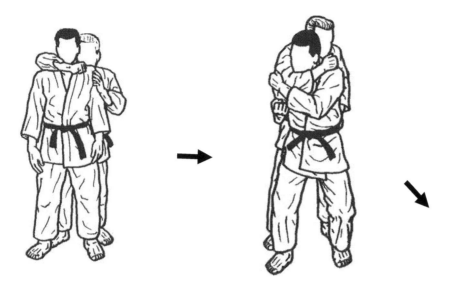

Mug 1 Tori
Stand in a natural position. As the adversary seizes you around the throat, turn your head into the bend of the adversary's arm and pull down with your left hand on his elbow. Strike Empi with your right elbow to his rib cage. Simultaneously bend your knees. Execute Ippon Seionage and throw the adversary to his side. Strike him to the head with Fomi Komi Geri and look for the next aggressor. Kiai throughout the technique.

Mug 1 Uke
Grab the defender around his neck. Kiai loudly. Your front should be on his back with no space in between. As you are thrown exhale and take a side fall.

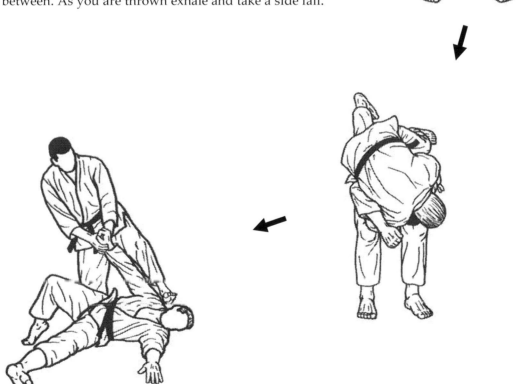

6th Kyu Orange Belt

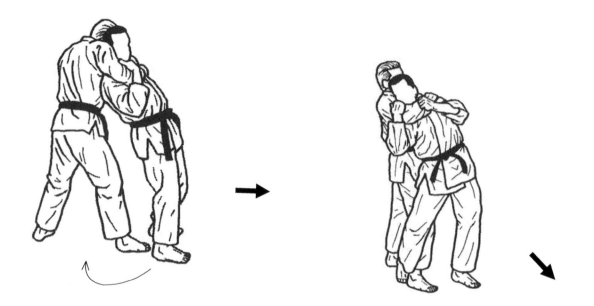

Mug 2 Tori

Stand in a natural position. The adversary's attack will pull your weight onto your heels. Turn your head into the bend of his arm. Reach up with both hands and grab his right arm. Draw a small semi-circle back with your right foot. This will trap the adversary's right leg. Pivot 180 degrees on your right leg. Step behind the adversary with your left leg and pull the adversary to his back. Strike with Fomi Komi Geri to his temple and look for the next aggressor. Kiai throughout the technique.

Mug 2 Uke

Grab the defender around his neck. Kiai loudly. Pull him slightly off balance by stepping back with your left leg. You will be thrown to your back, slap the mat and exhale.

Question 9- Weapons Attacks

Knife Stomach Thrust Kotegaeshi # 3   Tori
Stand in a relaxed natural position facing adversary. As adversary attacks inhale sharply, step forward with your left foot and pivot your hips 90 degrees clockwise. Bring your left hand up and over the adversary's attacking arm. Grab his arm at the wrist. Bring your other hand to meet his attacking hand. Pivot on your left foot; your hips should be against his hips. His elbow should be pressed tightly against your body. Pull the adversary around until he takes a step. Apply Kotegaeshi 3. Follow up with a ground control. Kiai throughout the technique.

Knife Stomach Thrust Kotegaeshi # 3 Uke
Execute a right thrust to the adversary's stomach. Kiai loudly. As you feel the pressure against your elbow (Kansetsuwaza), take a big step around with your left foot. Your wrist will be pushed towards your biceps. Prepare yourself for the Kotegaeshi free fall. Slap the mat vigorously when thrown and lie in a side fall position. Slap the mat again after you are taken to your stomach and immobilized.

6th Kyu Orange Belt

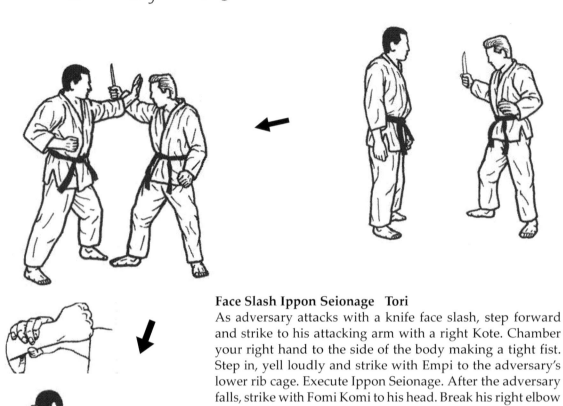

Face Slash Ippon Seionage   Tori

As adversary attacks with a knife face slash, step forward and strike to his attacking arm with a right Kote. Chamber your right hand to the side of the body making a tight fist. Step in, yell loudly and strike with Empi to the adversary's lower rib cage. Execute Ippon Seionage. After the adversary falls, strike with Fomi Komi to his head. Break his right elbow as you apply Kansetsuwaza pressure across your left shin with your left hand. Take the weapon with your right hand. Kiai throughout the technique.

Face Slash Ippon Seionage   Uke

Step forward with your right foot Execute a right face slash with a knife to the adversary's left cheek. Kiai as you slash. Exhale as you are struck in your rib cage. When the defender pivots into you there should be no space between your front and his back. Execute a side fall. Remember to exhale and slap the ground vigorously. Slap the ground again as you feel pressure against your elbow.

6th Kyu Orange Belt

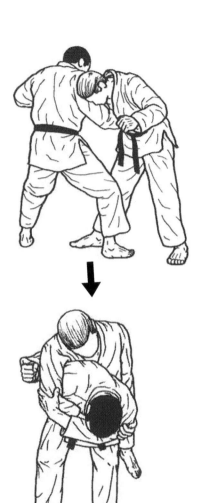

Club to the Side of the Head   Tori

As adversary attacks with a club to the side of the head, step forward and strike to his attacking arm with a left Kote. Chamber your right hand to the side of the body making a tight fist Immediately grab his arm. Step in, yell loudly and strike with Empi to the adversary's lower rib cage. Execute Ippon Seionage. After the adversary falls, strike with Fomi Komi to his head. Break his right elbow as you apply Kansetsuwaza pressure across your left shin with your left hand. Take the weapon with your right hand. Kiai throughout the technique.

Club to the Side of the Head   Uke

Step forward with your right foot. Execute a right strike to the head with a club. Kiai as you swing. Exhale as you are struck in your rib cage. When the defender pivots into you there should be no space between your front and his back. Execute a side fall. Remember to exhale and slap the ground vigorously. Slap the ground again as you feel pressure against your elbow.

Eight Points of Unbalance

Directly Forward

Directly Backward

Right Side

Left Side

**Right Corner
Forward**

**Right Corner
Backward**

**Left Corner
Forward**

**Left Corner
Backward**

Question 10 - Formal Throws

Ippon Seionage   Tori
Stand facing the Uke with your feet about shoulder width apart. Extend your right arm and grab his left lapel. Place your left hand under his right elbow. Break the Uke's balance forward. Step diagonally across with your right foot. Capture the adversary's armpit in the bend of your right elbow. Pivot on your right foot so that your back is to the adversary's front In order to gain leverage your waist should be below the adversary's waist. Bend forward at the waist and pull his right arm across your body. Rotate your shoulders pulling the adversary over your back. There is no audible Kiai on this technique but be sure to exhale.

Ippon Seionage   Uke
Grab the Tori's right lapel with your right hand and place your left hand under his right arm at the elbow. As he turns in relax and go up on your toes.Take a side fall and slap the mat. There is no audible Kiai on this technique but be sure to exhale.

Koshi Guruma   Tori

Stand facing the adversary, with your feet about shoulder width apart Extend your right arm and grab his left lapel. With your left hand grab under his right elbow. Step diagonally across with your right foot Pull the adversary's right arm at his elbow. Your right chest should touch his chest. This action will unbalance him to his right front comer. Simultaneously make a right Fist and reach around and grab the adversary's neck. Step in with your left foot bringing it behind your right foot. Your waist should be lower than your adversary's waist. Bend at the waist and pull the adversary over your hips. As you pull, tighten your abdomen. There is no audible Kiai on this technique, but be sure to exhale.

Koshi Guruma   Uke

Grab the Tori's right lapel with your right hand and place your left hand under his right arm at the elbow. As he turns in relax and go up on your toes. Take a side fall and slap the mat. There is no audible Kiai on this technique but be sure to exhale.

6th Kyu Orange Belt

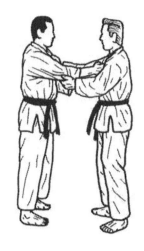

Uki Otoshi   Tori

Stand in a natural position. As Uke pushesgo with his movement. Pivot on your right foot, step back with your left leg. Turn counterclockwise, drop to your right knee, pulling the Uke's arm outward. Continue to pull the Uke's arm between his legs, forming a full circle. There is no audible Kiai during this technique.

Uki Otoshi   Uke

Push the Tori very aggressively with your right hand to his left shoulder. As the defender pulls let your momentum carry you. Raise your left leg in preparation for the free fall. Execute a free fall and slap the ground vigorously. There is no audible Kiai during this technique.

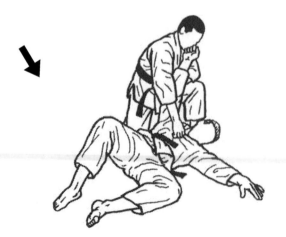

6th Kyu Orange Belt

Sonota Waza (Unofficial Techniques Taught at 6th Kyu)

Double Wrist Grab Juji Gatame   Tori

The adversary will grab you with both wrists while you are lying on your back. Grab his right hand with your right hand. Pivot to the side of your body and bring your right knee across his waist. Bring your left leg over his arm. Strike him to the face with a heel kick. Pull his arm across your body, bring him to his back and apply an elbow dislocation. After you dislocate his elbow immediately stand up.

Double Wrist Grab Juji Gatame   Uke

Grab both of the defender's wrists. You will be thrown to your back. When you feel pressure on your arm, slap the mat vigorously to indicate your submission.

6th Kyu Orange Belt

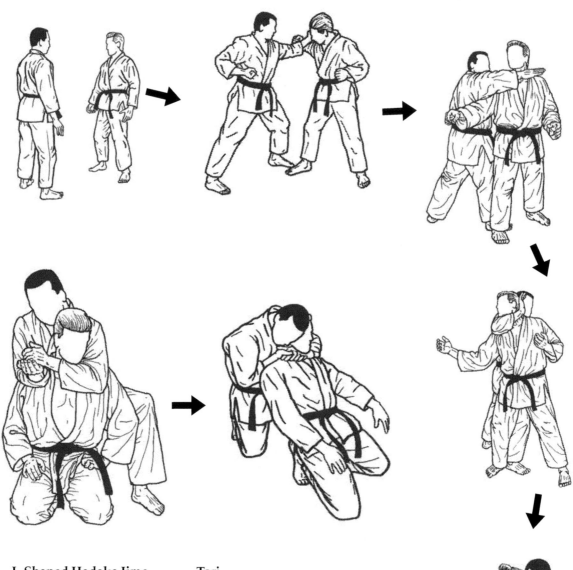

L-Shaped Hadaka Jime   Tori
Come directly behind the Uke who is in a kneeling postion.
Drop to your right knee. Place your right hand on top of
his shoulder palm up. Bend your wrist and make an L-
shape with your forearm against his back. Bring your left
fore arm across his throat with your wrist placed against
his throat. Push forward with your chest and pull back
with your arms. Place your head against the right side of
his head to control his head movement as you strangle
him.

L-Shaped Hadaka Jime   Uke
Assume a kneeling formal position. Slap the side of your
body when you feel pressure from the choke.

For illustrative purposes a defense against a punch with a
standing L- Shaped Hadaka jime is shown.

6th Kyu Orange Belt

Promotion Requirements for 5th Kyu Yellow Belt

5th Kyu Yellow Belt

Question 1 - Formal Bow and Ukemi

Formal Bow -Page 58

1a. Back Fall - Page 59

1b. Side Fall - One hand and two hands - Page 60

1b. Front Roll - Page 61

One Man Obstacle Roll

This roll is performed almost identically to the forward roll, except that you stretch upwards and jump in an arc. Stand with your right foot forward, right hand up in the air. Push off with your feet and roll along your pinkie finger, your arm and diagonally across your back. At no point should your head touch the ground. As you roll tuck the trailing leg in and perform a complete arc with the lead leg. On completion of your roll you should return to a standing position.

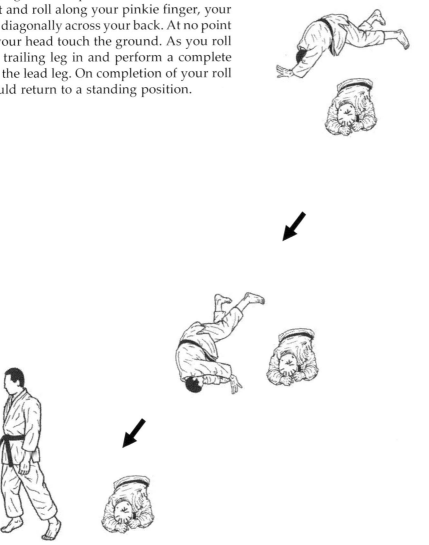

Question 2- Taisabaki

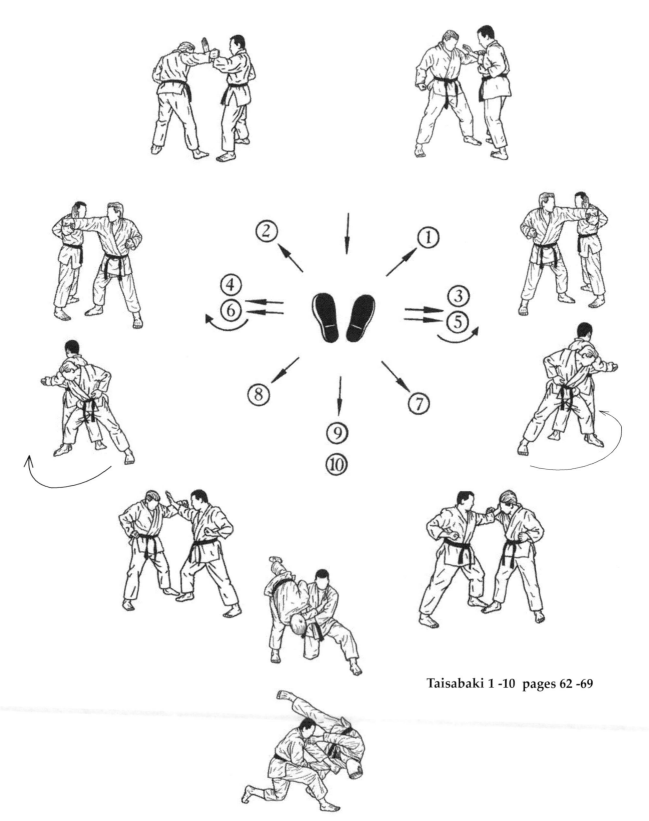

Taisabaki 1 -10 pages 62 -69

Question 3 - Kotegaeshi

3a. Kotegaeshi 1 page 70

3b. Kotegaeshi 2 page 71

3c. Kotegaeshi 3 page 72

5th Kyu Yellow Belt

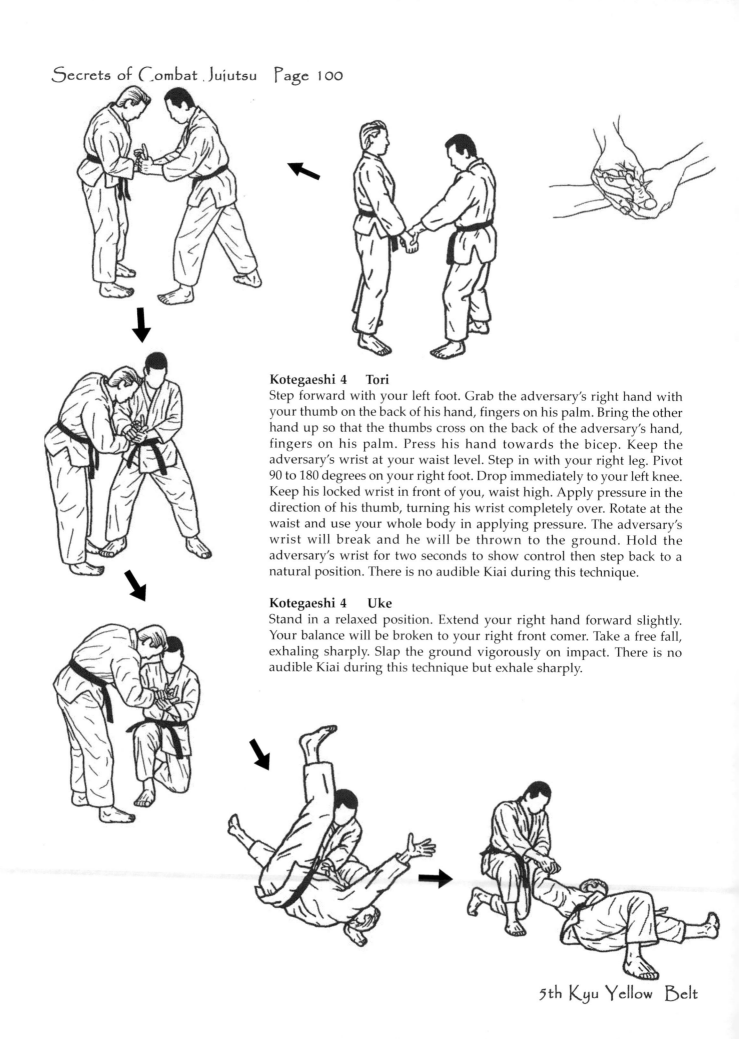

Kotegaeshi 4   Tori

Step forward with your left foot. Grab the adversary's right hand with your thumb on the back of his hand, fingers on his palm. Bring the other hand up so that the thumbs cross on the back of the adversary's hand, fingers on his palm. Press his hand towards the bicep. Keep the adversary's wrist at your waist level. Step in with your right leg. Pivot 90 to 180 degrees on your right foot. Drop immediately to your left knee. Keep his locked wrist in front of you, waist high. Apply pressure in the direction of his thumb, turning his wrist completely over. Rotate at the waist and use your whole body in applying pressure. The adversary's wrist will break and he will be thrown to the ground. Hold the adversary's wrist for two seconds to show control then step back to a natural position. There is no audible Kiai during this technique.

Kotegaeshi 4   Uke

Stand in a relaxed position. Extend your right hand forward slightly. Your balance will be broken to your right front comer. Take a free fall, exhaling sharply. Slap the ground vigorously on impact. There is no audible Kiai during this technique but exhale sharply.

5th Kyu Yellow Belt

Question 4- Kansetsuwaza Page 73

Question 5 - Wrist Grabs

5a. Double Wrist Grab Kansetsuwaza   page 74

5b. Single Wrist Grab Kansetsuwaza page 76

5a. Double Wrist Grab Kotegaeshi page 75

5b. Single Wrist Grab Kotegaeshi page 77

5th Kyu Yellow Belt

Single Cross Wrist Grab Kansetsuwaza Tori
Stand in a relaxed natural position. The adversary will grab your right wrist with his right hand. Grab his right wrist by turning your hand clockwise around his wrist. Strike left Mae Geri to his knee. Step in left foot and apply Kansetsuwaza to the adversary's elbow. Bring him to the ground strongly and immobilize him with your ground control. Kiai throughout the technique.

Single Cross Wrist Grab Kansetsuwaza Uke
Grab the defender's right wrist aggressively with your right hand. Kiai loudly. When kicked draw your attention to your knee. As your elbow is locked, bend forward slightly. Slap the side of your body as you feel pressure on your elbow. You will be fully unbalanced at this point and unable to step. Fall forward, turning your head away from the captured arm. This will alleviate the pressure. Slap the mat vigorously when you feel pressure on your shoulder.

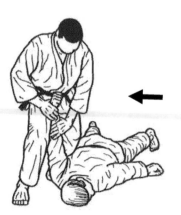

Single Cross Wrist Grab Kotegaeshi   Tori
Stand in a relaxed natural position. The adversary will grab your right wrist with his right hand. Kick to his knee with a right Mae Geri as you grab his right wrist. Step down and apply Kotegaeshi 3. Strike the adversary with Fomi Komi Geri to the temple. Twist the adversary's wrist towards the knife edge of his hand until he turns to his face. Immobilize him by locking his arm with Kansetsuwaza. Kiai throughout the technique.

Single Cross Wrist Grab Kotegaeshi   Uke
Grab the defender's right wrist with your right hand. Kiai loudly. When you are kicked in the knee direct your attention to your knee. Simulate being struck and allow the Tori to turn your wrist. Execute a free fall. Relax and go with the wrist turning action. Slap when you feel pressure on your shoulder.

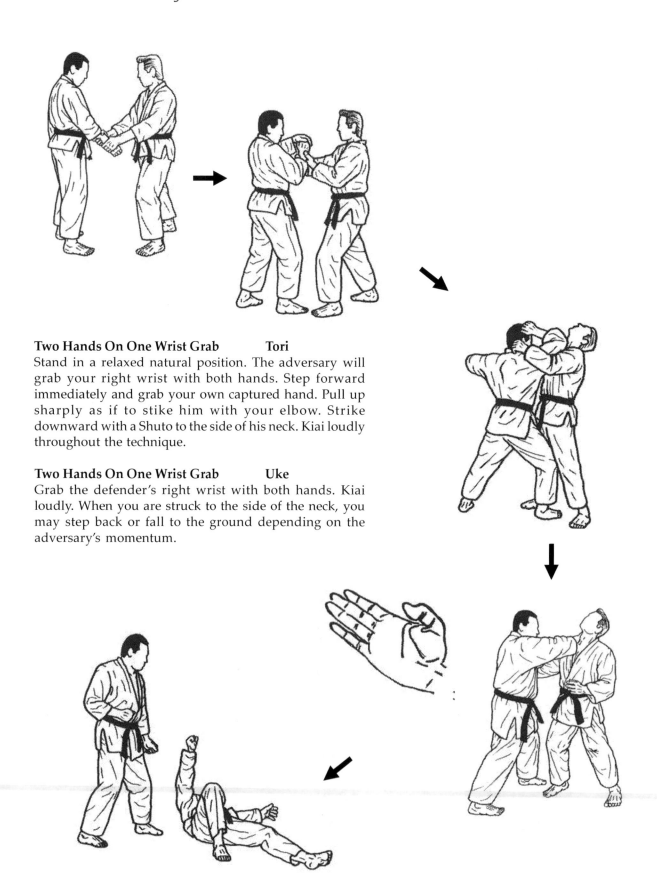

Two Hands On One Wrist Grab   Tori
Stand in a relaxed natural position. The adversary will grab your right wrist with both hands. Step forward immediately and grab your own captured hand. Pull up sharply as if to stike him with your elbow. Strike downward with a Shuto to the side of his neck. Kiai loudly throughout the technique.

Two Hands On One Wrist Grab   Uke
Grab the defender's right wrist with both hands. Kiai loudly. When you are struck to the side of the neck, you may step back or fall to the ground depending on the adversary's momentum.

Question 6 - Lapel Grabs

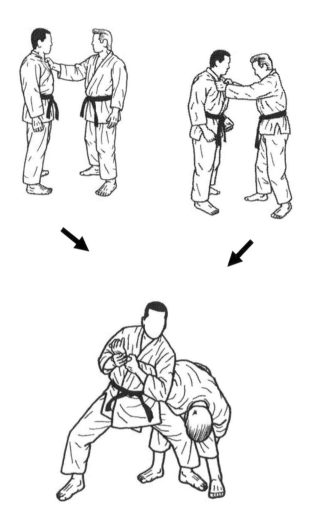

6a. Single Lapel Grab Kansetsuwaza page 80

6b. Double Lapel Grab Kansetsuwaza page 78

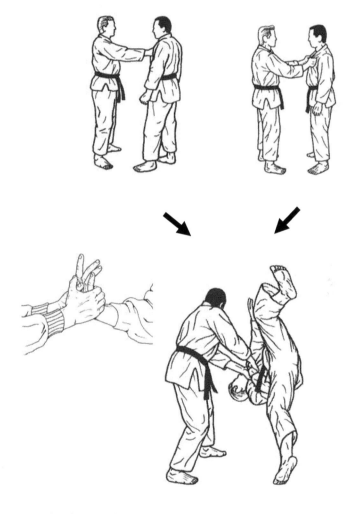

6a. Single Lapel Grab Kotegaeshi   page 81

6b. Double Lapel Grab Kotegaeshi   page 79

Single Lapel Pull Close   Tori
Stand in a natural position. The adversary will grab you by your lapel and pull you in close. Go with the pull. Step forward with your left leg. Grab his right wrist with your left hand and his right elbow with your right hand. Off-balance him to his right rear corner and apply Osotogari. Strike him on the ground and break his elbow across your knee. Kiai loudly throughout the technique.

Single Lapel Pull Close   Uke
Grab the defender by his left lapel and pull him forward. Kiai loudly. You will be off-balanced to your right rear corner and then thrown to your back. Slap when you feel pressure on your elbow.

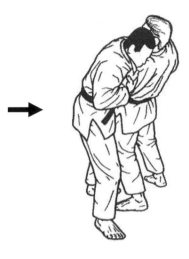

Single Lapel Pull Close Tori
Stand in a natural position. The adversary will grab you by your lapel and pull you in close. Go with the pull. Step forward with your right leg. Grab his left wrist with your right hand and his left elbow with your left hand. Off-balance him to his left rear corner with Ude Garami and throw him down. (There is no need to reap him). Strike him on the ground and break his elbow across your knee. Kiai loudly throughout the technique.

Single Lapel Pull Close Uke
Grab the defender by his right lapel and pull him forward. Kiai loudly. You will be off-balanced to your left rear corner and then thrown to your back. Slap when you feel pressure on your elbow.

Question 7 - Body Grabs from Behind

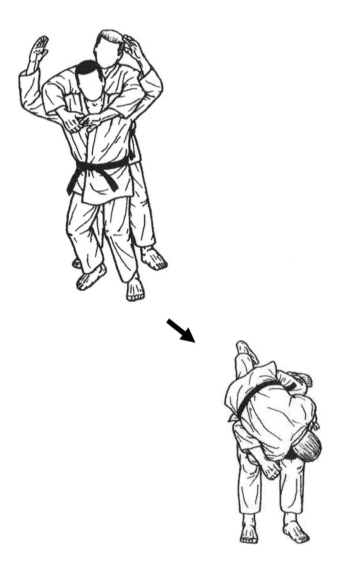

7a. Upper chest grab page 82

Rear lower arms   Tori
Stand in a natural position. The adversary will seize you aggressively around your chest with both arms below your elbows. Step out with your left leg and strike to the adversary's groin. Grab the groin, step behind his leg and throw the adversary to his back in a scooping motion. Strike to the adversary's head with Fomi Komi Geri. Immediately look for another aggressor. Kiai throughout the technique.

Rear lower arms   Uke
Grab the defender tightly around his body. Kiai loudly. Your arms should be below his elbows and there should be no space between you and the defender. The defender will grab your right thigh in class and throw you to your back.

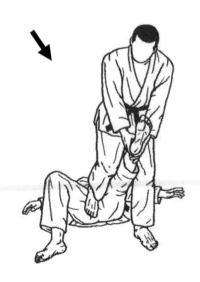

Rear under arms   Tori

Stand in a natural position. The adversary will seize you aggressively around your chest under both arms. Step out with your right foot and strike Empi to the adversary's head. Reach down between your legs and grab his left ankle with both hands. Pull up; apply pressure with the adversary's knee against your thigh and throw him to his back. Strike the adversary on the ground to his groin with Fomi Komi Geri. Kiai throughout the technique.

Rear under arms   Uke

Grab the adversary tightly around his chest under his arms. Kiai loudly. Move your head to simulate that you have been struck. Take a back fall and exhale sharply.

Question 8 - Mugs

8a. Mug 1 page 83

8a. Mug 2 page 84

Mug 3   Tori

Stand in a natural position. The adversary's attack will pull your weight completely onto your heels. Reach up and grab as high as you can with your right hand. Pivot 90-180 degrees to your left on your right leg so that your left knee ends up between his legs. Place your left hand on the ground so that the adversary has some room to fall (this is a class time safety measure). Bring your right knee to meet your left knee. Throw the adversary to his back and strike Seiken to the adversary's face. Kiai throughout the technique.

Mug 3   Uke

Grab the defender and pull him back onto his heels. Kiai loudly. Take a back fall as you are thrown over his back.

Question 9 - Weapon Attacks

9a. Stomach thrust page 85

9b. Face slash page 86

9c. Club Strike page 87

5th Kyu Yellow Belt

Carotid stab Tori

Stand in a natural position. The adversary lunges with an overhead knife attack to your carotid artery. Step with your right foot diagonally across your body. Raise your arm and deflect the oncoming arm. Pivot on your right foot stepping forward with your left foot. Strike with a slap to the back of his head. Pivot 180 degrees clockwise on your left foot. Brace the adversary's arm against your side with both hands and apply pressure to his elbow. Pull his arm between your legs and force him to take a step. Before he places his foot execute Kotegaeshi 3. Turn his wrist towards the knife edge of his hand until he turns to a prostrate position. Immobilize him with a ground control and continue to apply pressure until you have removed the knife. Kiai throughout the technique.

Carotid stab Uke

Stab at the defender in an overhead manner. Kiai loudly. As the defender braces your elbow take a step then immediately execute a free fall. Slap the mat when you feel pressure against your shoulder.

Club to the Top of the Head   Tori

Stand in a natural position. The adversary lunges with a club attack to the top of your head. Step with your right foot diagonally across your body. Raise your arm and deflect the oncoming arm. Pivot on your right foot stepping forward with your left foot. Strike with a slap to the back of his head. Pivot 180 degrees clockwise on your left foot. Brace the adversary's arm against you side with both hands and apply pressure to his elbow. Pull his arm across your body and force him to take a step. Before he places his foot, execute Kotegaeshi 3. Turn his wrist towards the knife edge of his hand until he turns to a prostrate position. Immobilize him with a ground control and continue to apply pressure until you have removed the knife. Kiai loudly throughout the technique.

Carotid to the Top of the Head   Uke

Strike at the defender in an overhead manner. Kiai loudly. As the defender braces your elbow take a step then immediately execute a free fall. Slap the mat when you feel pressure against your shoulder.

5th Kyu Yellow Belt

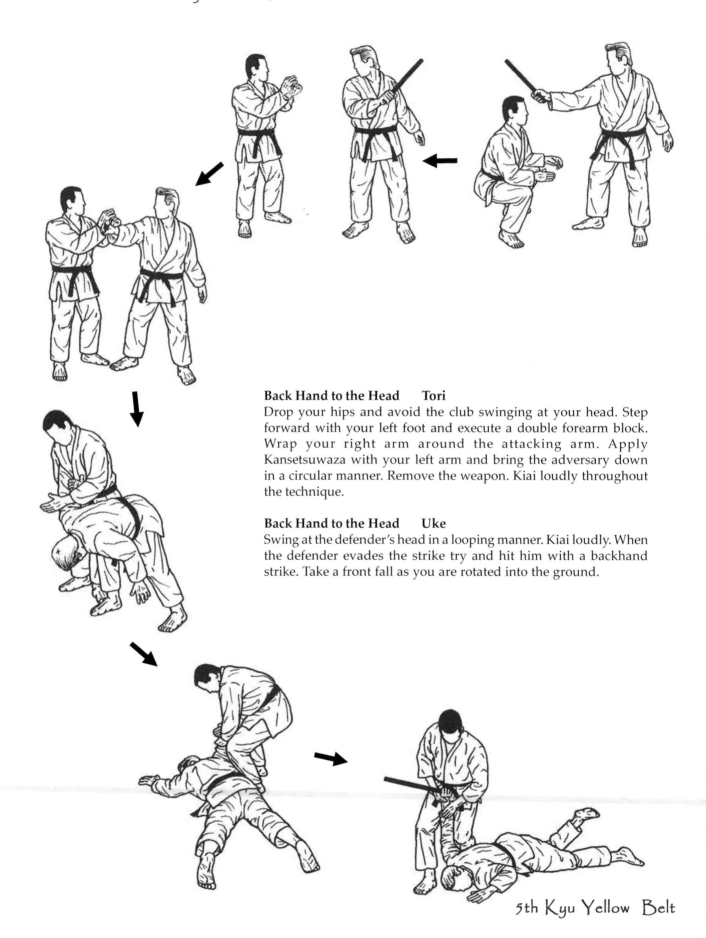

Back Hand to the Head   Tori
Drop your hips and avoid the club swinging at your head. Step forward with your left foot and execute a double forearm block. Wrap your right arm around the attacking arm. Apply Kansetsuwaza with your left arm and bring the adversary down in a circular manner. Remove the weapon. Kiai loudly throughout the technique.

Back Hand to the Head   Uke
Swing at the defender's head in a looping manner. Kiai loudly. When the defender evades the strike try and hit him with a backhand strike. Take a front fall as you are rotated into the ground.

5th Kyu Yellow Belt

Question 10 - Formal Throws

10a. Ippon Seionage page 90

10b. Koshi Guruma page 91

10c. Uki Otoshi page 92

Osotogari   Tori
Stand facing the Uke, with your feet about shoulder width apart. Extend your right arm and grab his left lapel. Place your left hand grab under his right elbow. Step in with your left foot and off-balance the adversary to his right rear corner by turning your arms in a circular fashion. Bring your right leg forward and reap behind the adversary's right leg. The adversary will be thrown to his back. There is no audible kiai in this technique.

Osotogari   Uke
Stand facing the Tori in a right sided formal position. Your weight will be unbalanced to your right rear corner. Take a side fall to the rear. There is no audible kiai in this technique.

Sukuinage   **Tori**

Stand facing the adversary, with your feet about shoulder width apart. Extend your right arm and grab his left lapel. Place your left hand grab under his right elbow. Step to his left side with your right foot. Bring your left foot to meet your right foot, and then step behind the adversary. Grab behind the adversary's knees, pick him up and throw him with your body. As the adversary falls step back with your right foot. There is no audible Kiai in this technique.

Sukuinage   **Uke**

Stand in a right sided formal postion. You will take a high back fall so exhale sharply. There is no audible Kiai in this technique.

5th Kyu Yellow Belt

Sonota Waza (Unofficial Techniques Taught At 5th Kyu)

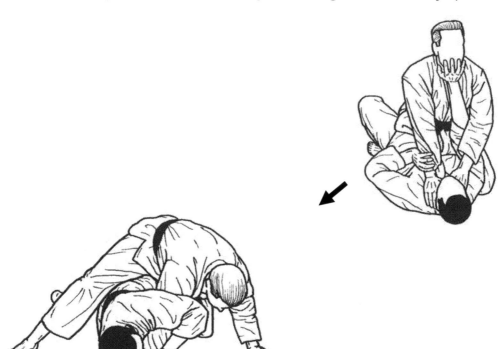

Double Hand Choke Kansetsuwaza   Tori
The adversary will grab you in a two hand choke hold while you are lying on your back. Grab his right hand with your left hand. Strike to his face forcing his head back. Pivot to your right side. Roll on his arm and apply an elbow dislocation. After you dislocate his elbow immediately stand up.

Double Hand Choke Kansetsuwaza   Uke
Grab the defender in a two handed choke. When you feel pressure on your arm, slap the mat vigorously to indicate your submission.

5th Kyu Yellow Belt

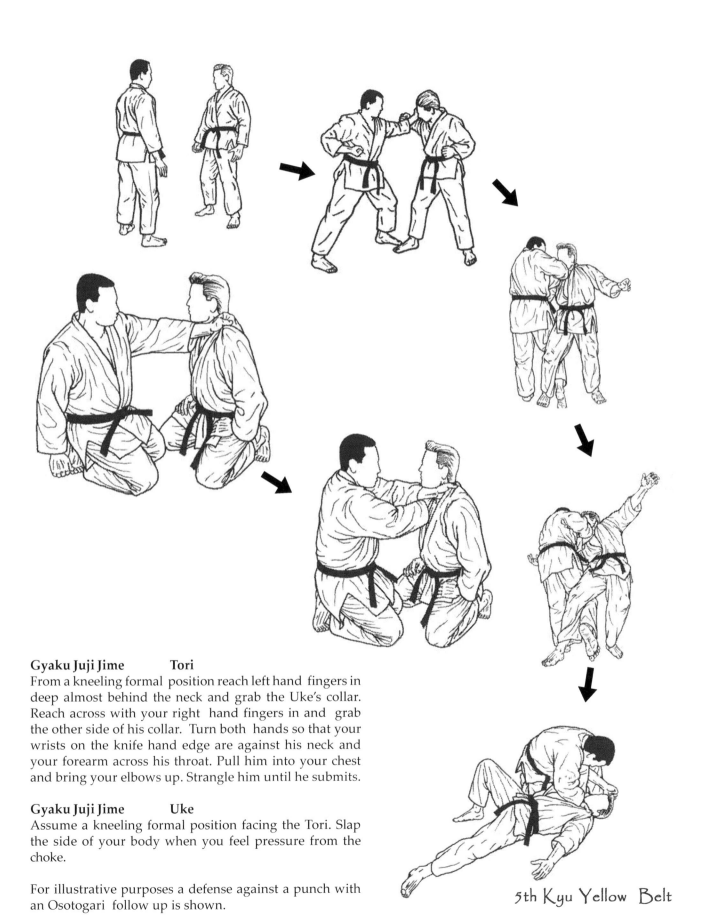

Gyaku Juji Jime   Tori

From a kneeling formal position reach left hand fingers in deep almost behind the neck and grab the Uke's collar. Reach across with your right hand fingers in and grab the other side of his collar. Turn both hands so that your wrists on the knife hand edge are against his neck and your forearm across his throat. Pull him into your chest and bring your elbows up. Strangle him until he submits.

Gyaku Juji Jime   Uke

Assume a kneeling formal position facing the Tori. Slap the side of your body when you feel pressure from the choke.

For illustrative purposes a defense against a punch with an Osotogari follow up is shown.

5th Kyu Yellow Belt

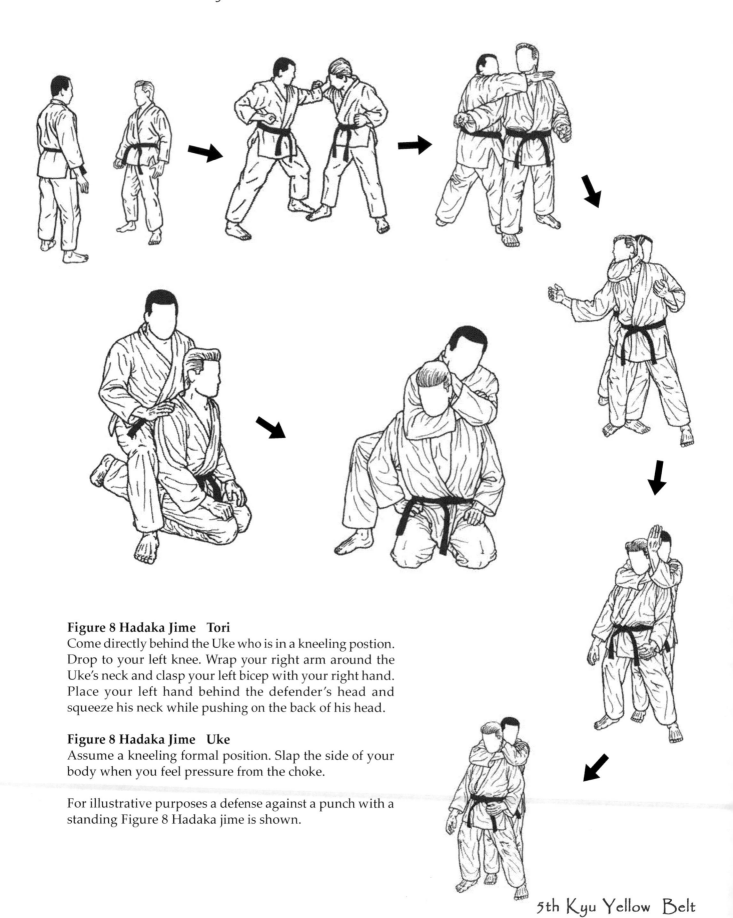

Figure 8 Hadaka Jime   Tori
Come directly behind the Uke who is in a kneeling postion. Drop to your left knee. Wrap your right arm around the Uke's neck and clasp your left bicep with your right hand. Place your left hand behind the defender's head and squeeze his neck while pushing on the back of his head.

Figure 8 Hadaka Jime   Uke
Assume a kneeling formal position. Slap the side of your body when you feel pressure from the choke.

For illustrative purposes a defense against a punch with a standing Figure 8 Hadaka jime is shown.

5th Kyu Yellow Belt

Nami Juji Jime

Gyaku Juji Jime

Kata Juji Jime

Nami Juji Jime Tori
From a kneeling formal position reach left hand thumb in deep almost behind the neck and grab the Uke's collar. Reach across with your right hand thumb in and grab the other side of his collar. Turn both hands so that your wrists on the knife hand edge are against his neck and your forearm across his throat. Pull him into your chest and bring your elbows up. Strangle him until he submits.

Nami Juji Jime Uke
Assume a kneeling formal position facing the Tori. Slap the side of your body when you feel pressure from the choke.

Promotion Requirements for 4th Kyu Green Belt

4th Kyu Green Belt

Question 1 - Formal Bow and Ukemi

Formal Bow - page 58

1a. Back Fall - page 59

1b. Side Fall - One hand and two hands - page 60

1c. Front Roll - page 61

Forward somersault

Stand in a natural position (Shizentai kamae). Hands hang loosely at the side. Spread both feet about 1 ½ times your shoulder width. Place both fists on the ground. Your hands should be the same distance as your feet. Push off on both fists. Perform a somersault. Tuck your head in, do not let it touch the ground. On impact, tighten your abdomen and exhale sharply. Slap with the hands. Arch your back so that the only parts of your body that make contact on impact are the balls of the feet, the shoulders, and the hands. Your neck and head should not make contact with the ground. This fall can be performed with or without hands.

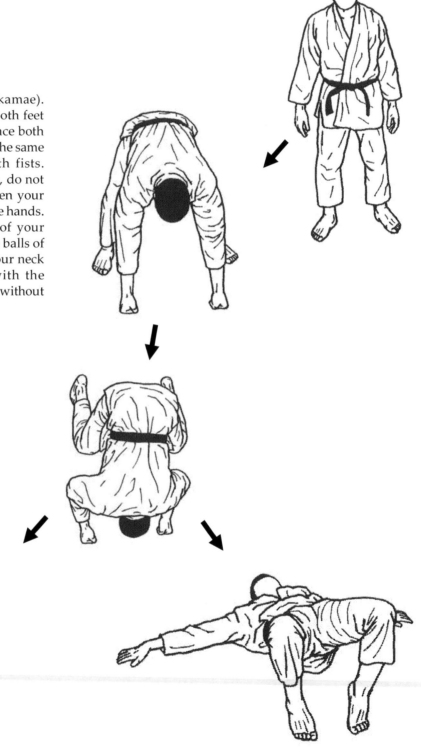

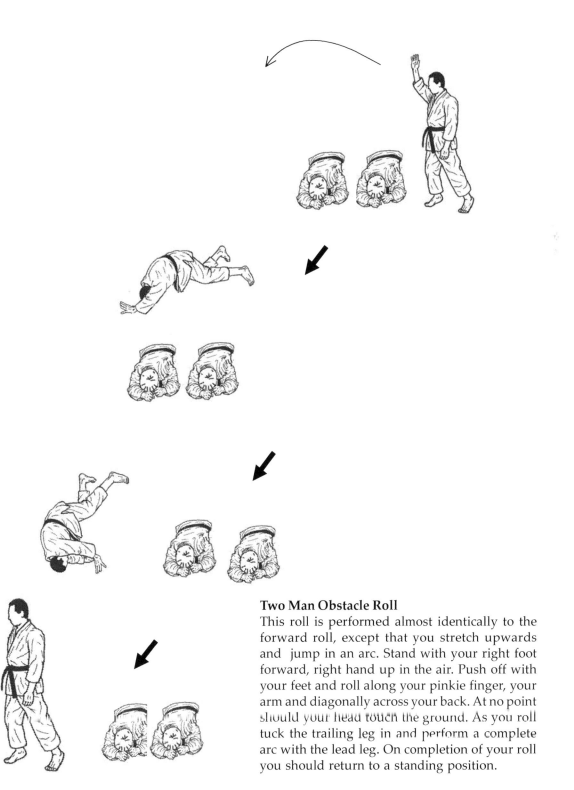

Two Man Obstacle Roll
This roll is performed almost identically to the forward roll, except that you stretch upwards and jump in an arc. Stand with your right foot forward, right hand up in the air. Push off with your feet and roll along your pinkie finger, your arm and diagonally across your back. At no point should your head touch the ground. As you roll tuck the trailing leg in and perform a complete arc with the lead leg. On completion of your roll you should return to a standing position.

Question 2- Taisabaki

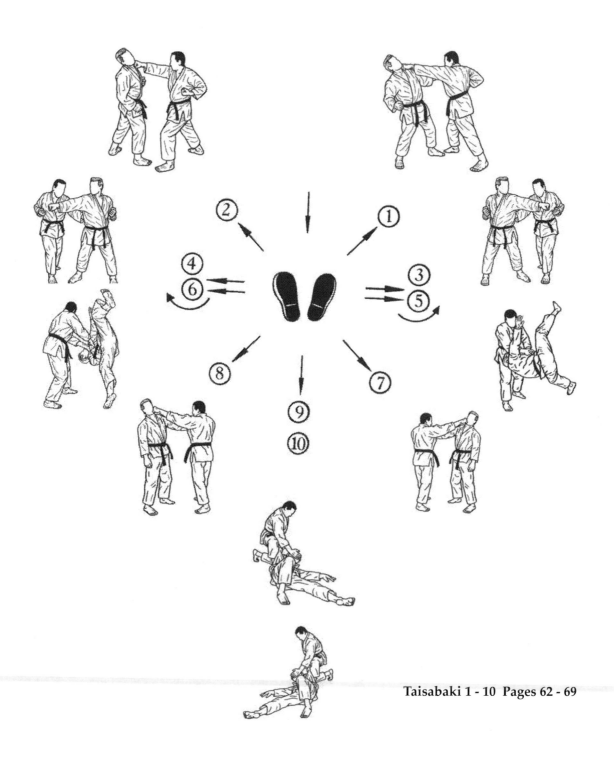

Taisabaki 1 - 10 Pages 62 - 69

Question 2b - What is Atemi Waza (Striking Techniques)
Question 2c- Name four hand techniques used in Atemi Waza

Seiken (fore-fist)
Curl the fingers at the second joint. Then curl them again at the knuckles. Place your thumb over the fingers. This action makes a fist tight. Strike with the front two knuckles of the fore-fist.
Targets: face/ chin, temple, ear, solar plexus, abdomen, ribs, groin, and kidney.

Tateken (vertical fist)
Curl the fingers at the second joint, and then curl them again at the knuckles. Place your thumb over the fingers. This action makes a tight fist. The striking surface is the first two knuckles and the fore fist. Targets: face, chin, temple, ear, solar plexus, abdomen, ribs, spleen, groin.

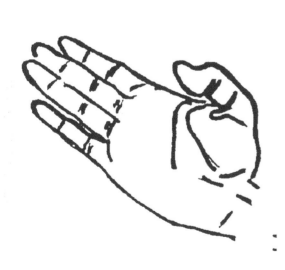

Shuto (Knife Hand)
Open your hand. Extend your fingers pressing them together. Bend your thumb and tuck it against your hand.
The striking surface is the knife edge of the hand.
Targets: nose, throat, collarbone, abdomen, ribs, spleen, groin.

Shotei (Heel Palm)
Extend your fingers and push your palm out. Bend your thumb and tuck it against your hand. The striking surface is the heel of the palm. Targets: face, chin, temple, ear, solar plexus, abdomen, ribs, spleen, groin.

Question 3 - Kotegaeshi

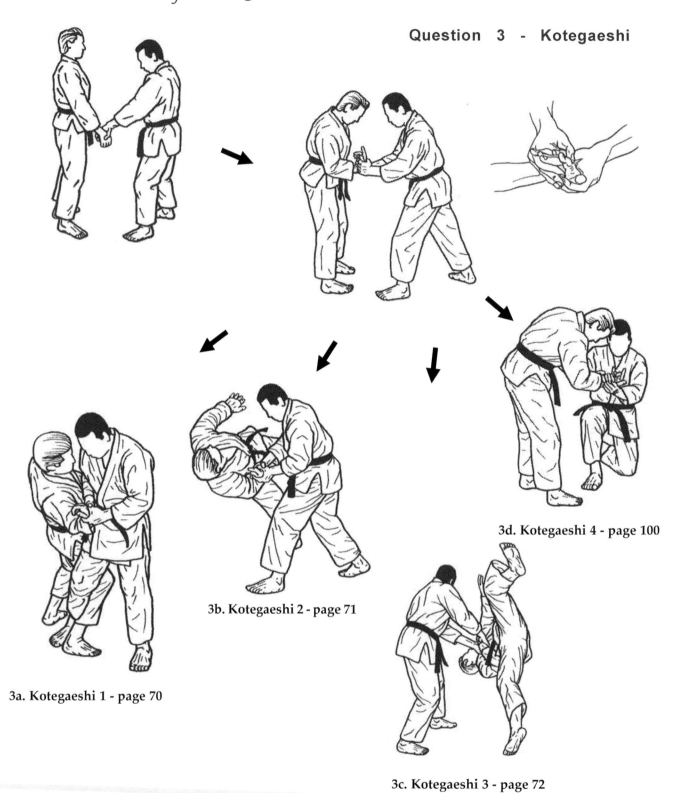

3a. Kotegaeshi 1 - page 70

3b. Kotegaeshi 2 - page 71

3c. Kotegaeshi 3 - page 72

3d. Kotegaeshi 4 - page 100

Question 3 - Kotegaeshi

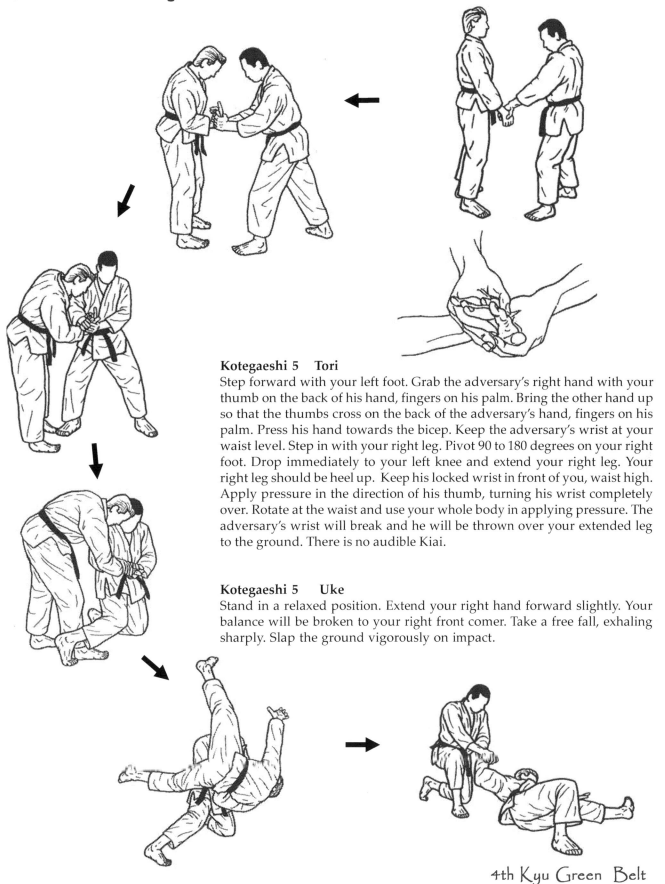

Kotegaeshi 5   Tori
Step forward with your left foot. Grab the adversary's right hand with your thumb on the back of his hand, fingers on his palm. Bring the other hand up so that the thumbs cross on the back of the adversary's hand, fingers on his palm. Press his hand towards the bicep. Keep the adversary's wrist at your waist level. Step in with your right leg. Pivot 90 to 180 degrees on your right foot. Drop immediately to your left knee and extend your right leg. Your right leg should be heel up. Keep his locked wrist in front of you, waist high. Apply pressure in the direction of his thumb, turning his wrist completely over. Rotate at the waist and use your whole body in applying pressure. The adversary's wrist will break and he will be thrown over your extended leg to the ground. There is no audible Kiai.

Kotegaeshi 5   Uke
Stand in a relaxed position. Extend your right hand forward slightly. Your balance will be broken to your right front comer. Take a free fall, exhaling sharply. Slap the ground vigorously on impact.

4th Kyu Green Belt

Question 4 Kansetsuwaza
Question 4a. Single Wrist   Grab Page 76

Elbow Grab Kansetsuwaza   Tori

Stand in a relaxed natural position. The adversary will grab your left elbow with his right hand. Bring your left hand up and trap his right hand in the bend in your elbow. Strike Seiken to a vital point on the adversary's face. Step in left foot and apply Kansetsuwaza to the adversary's elbow. Bring him to the ground strongly and immobilize him with your ground control. Kiai throughout the technique.

Elbow Grab Kansetsuwaza   Uke

Grab the defender's left elbow aggressively with your right hand. Kiai loudly. Move your head back to simulate being struck. As your elbow is locked, bend forward slightly. Slap the side of your body as you feel pressure on your elbow. You will be fully unbalanced at this point and unable to step. Fall forward turning your head away from the captured arm. This will alleviate the pressure. Slap the mat vigorously when you feel pressure on your shoulder.

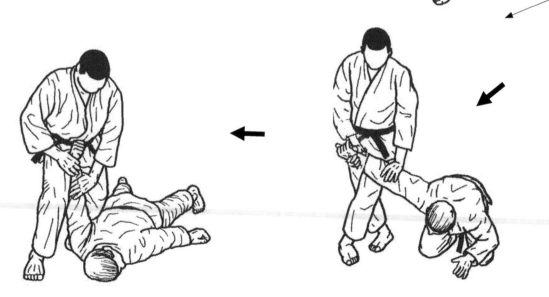

4th Kyu Green Belt

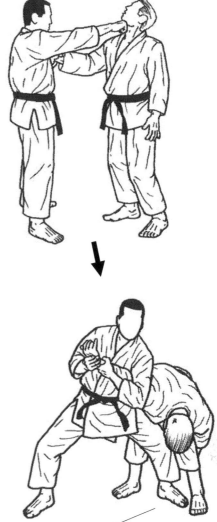

Shoulder Grab Kansetsuwaza Tori

Stand in a relaxed natural position. The adversary will grab your left shoulder with his right hand. Bring your left hand up and trap his right hand. Strike Seiken to a vital point on the adversary's face. Step in left foot and apply Kansetsuwaza to the adversary's elbow. Bring him to the ground strongly and immobilize him with your ground control. Kiai throughout the technique.

Shoulder Grab Kansetsuwaza Uke

Grab the defender's left shoulder aggressively with your right hand. Kiai loudly. Move your head back to simulate being struck. As your elbow is locked, bend forward slightly. Slap the side of your body as you feel pressure on your elbow. You will be fully unbalanced at this point and unable to step. Fall forward turning your head away from the captured arm. This will alleviate the pressure. Slap the mat vigorously when you feel pressure on your shoulder.

Question 5   Wrist Grabs

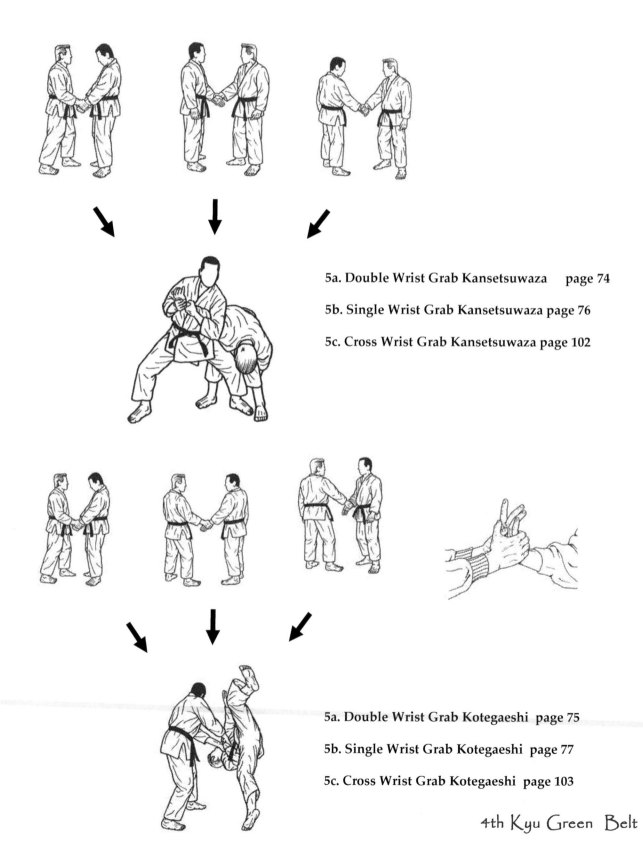

5a. Double Wrist Grab Kansetsuwaza   page 74

5b. Single Wrist Grab Kansetsuwaza page 76

5c. Cross Wrist Grab Kansetsuwaza page 102

5a. Double Wrist Grab Kotegaeshi page 75

5b. Single Wrist Grab Kotegaeshi page 77

5c. Cross Wrist Grab Kotegaeshi page 103

4th Kyu Green Belt

Two Hands On One Wrist Grab   Tori
Stand in a relaxed natural position. The adversary will grab your right wrist with both hands. Srike to his face with Uraken and Kiai loudly. Step back with your right leg, turning your body 90 degrees and pulling him sharply off balance to the front. Bring the right arm up and throw him with Irimi Nage. It does not matter if he holds on or not. Kiai throughout the technique.

Two Hands On One Wrist Grab   Uke
Grab the defender's right wrist with both hands. Kiai loudly. Loosen up your grip to simulate being struck. Go with the defender as he pulls you forward and then fall to your back with the Irimi Nage throw.

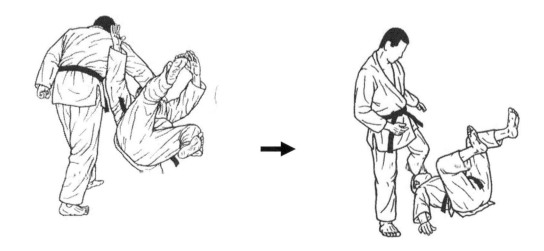

Question 6 - Lapel Grabs

6b. Double Lapel Grab Kansetsuwaza   page 78

6b. Double Lapel Grab Kotegaeshi page 79

6c. Single Pull Close Osotogari page 106

6d. Single Pull Close Ude Garami page 107

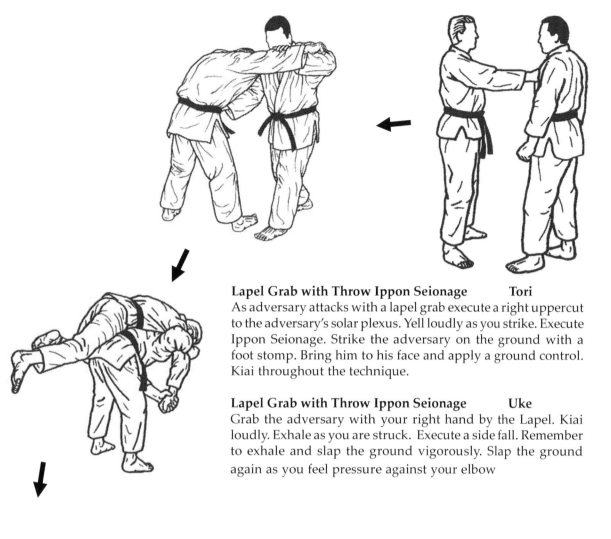

Lapel Grab with Throw Ippon Seionage   Tori
As adversary attacks with a lapel grab execute a right uppercut to the adversary's solar plexus. Yell loudly as you strike. Execute Ippon Seionage. Strike the adversary on the ground with a foot stomp. Bring him to his face and apply a ground control. Kiai throughout the technique.

Lapel Grab with Throw Ippon Seionage   Uke
Grab the adversary with your right hand by the Lapel. Kiai loudly. Exhale as you are struck. Execute a side fall. Remember to exhale and slap the ground vigorously. Slap the ground again as you feel pressure against your elbow

4th Kyu Green Belt

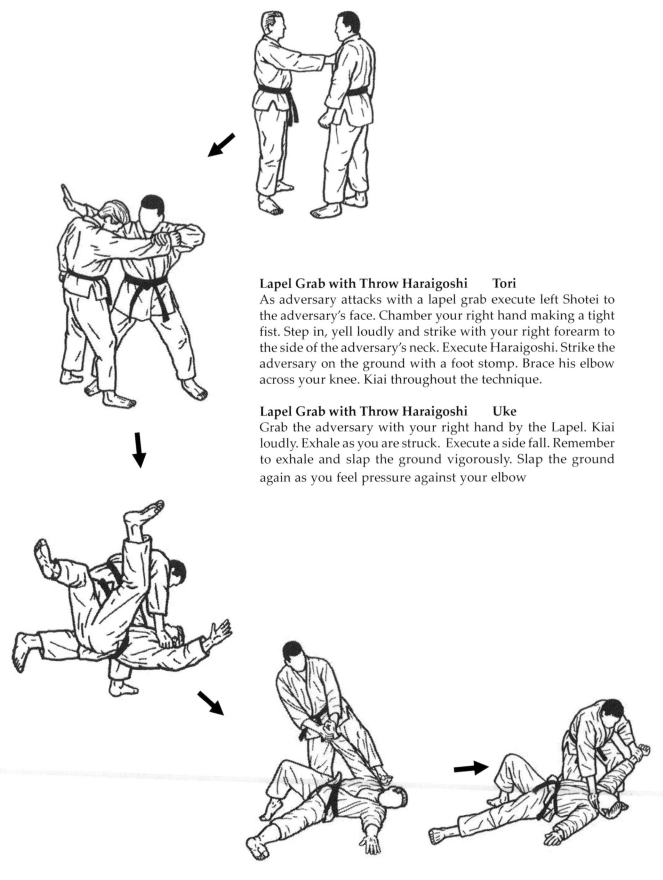

Lapel Grab with Throw Haraigoshi   Tori
As adversary attacks with a lapel grab execute left Shotei to the adversary's face. Chamber your right hand making a tight fist. Step in, yell loudly and strike with your right forearm to the side of the adversary's neck. Execute Haraigoshi. Strike the adversary on the ground with a foot stomp. Brace his elbow across your knee. Kiai throughout the technique.

Lapel Grab with Throw Haraigoshi   Uke
Grab the adversary with your right hand by the Lapel. Kiai loudly. Exhale as you are struck. Execute a side fall. Remember to exhale and slap the ground vigorously. Slap the ground again as you feel pressure against your elbow

Cross Lapel Grab Kotegaeshi — Tori

Stand in a relaxed natural position. The adversary will grab your right lapel with his right hand. Turn your left hand up, palm facing towards you and grab the back of his right hand. Simultaneously strike to the side of his head. Step down and apply Kotegaeshi 3. Strike the adversary with Fomi Komi Geri to the temple. Twist the adversary's wrist towards the knife edge of his hand until he turns to his face. Immobilize him by locking his arm with Kansetsuwaza. Kiai throughout the technique.

Cross Lapel Grab Kotegaeshi — Uke

Grab the defender's right lapel with your right hand. Kiai loudly. When you are slapped in the head relax your grip. Simulate being struck and allow the Tori to turn your wrist. Execute a free fall. Relax and go with the wrist turning action. Slap when you feel pressure on your shoulder.

Cross Lapel Grab Kansetsuwaza   Tori

Stand in a relaxed natural position. The adversary will grab your right lapel with his right hand. Bring your left hand up and trap his right hand. Strike Seiken to a vital point on the adversary's face. Step in left foot and apply Kansetsuwaza to the adversary's elbow. Bring him to the ground strongly and immobilize him with your ground control. Kiai throughout the technique.

Shoulder Grab Kansetsuwaza Uke

Grab the defender's right lapel aggressively with your right hand. Kiai loudly. Move your head back to simulate being struck. As your elbow is locked, bend forward slightly. Slap the side of your body as you feel pressure on your elbow. You will be fully unbalanced at this point and unable to step. Fall forward turning your head away from the captured arm. This will alleviate the pressure. Slap the mat vigorously when you feel pressure on your shoulder.

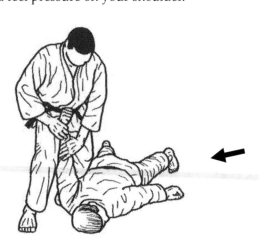

Question 7 - Body Grabs From Behind

7a. Upper Chest Grab   page 82

7b. Lower Chest Grab   page 109

7c. Under Arms Chest Grab   page 110

Rear Under Arms   Tori
Stand in a natural position. The adversary will seize you aggressively around your chest under both arms. Strike the adversary with your left elbow. Reach down and grab both of the adversary's ankles. Pull up and throw the adversary to his back. Strike the adversary on the ground to his groin with Fumi Komi Geri. Turn and look for the next aggressor. Kiai throughout the technique.

Rear Under Arms   Uke
Grab the adversary tightly around his chest under his arms. Move your head to simulate that you have been struck. Take a back fall and Kiai throughout the technique.

4th Kyu Green Belt

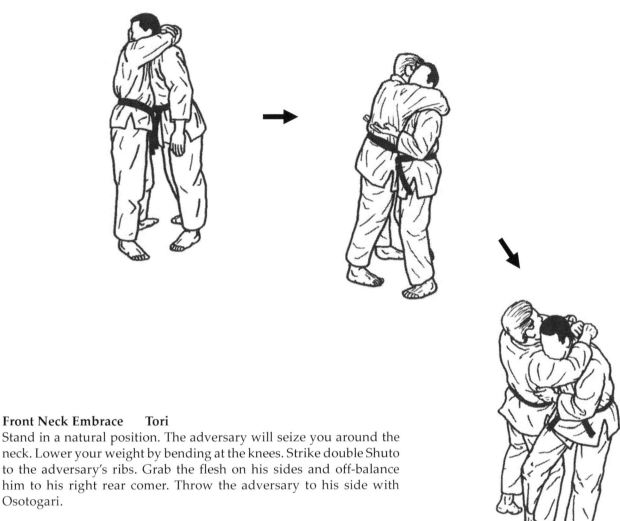

Front Neck Embrace   Tori
Stand in a natural position. The adversary will seize you around the neck. Lower your weight by bending at the knees. Strike double Shuto to the adversary's ribs. Grab the flesh on his sides and off-balance him to his right rear comer. Throw the adversary to his side with Osotogari.

Front Neck Embrace   Uke
Grab the defender around his neck. Simulate being struck in the ribs and loosen your hold. Take a side fall.

Chest embrace Tori
Stand in a natural position. The adversary will seize you under your arms and around your chest. Lower your weight by bending at the knees. Slap double Shotei to the adversary's ears. Throw the adversary to his back with Koshi Guruma. Strike to his head with Fomi Komi Geri.

Chest embrace Uke
Grab the defender under his arms and around his chest. Simulate being slapped in the ears. Take a free fall. React as if you were hit in the face. Tap out when you feel pressure on your elbow.

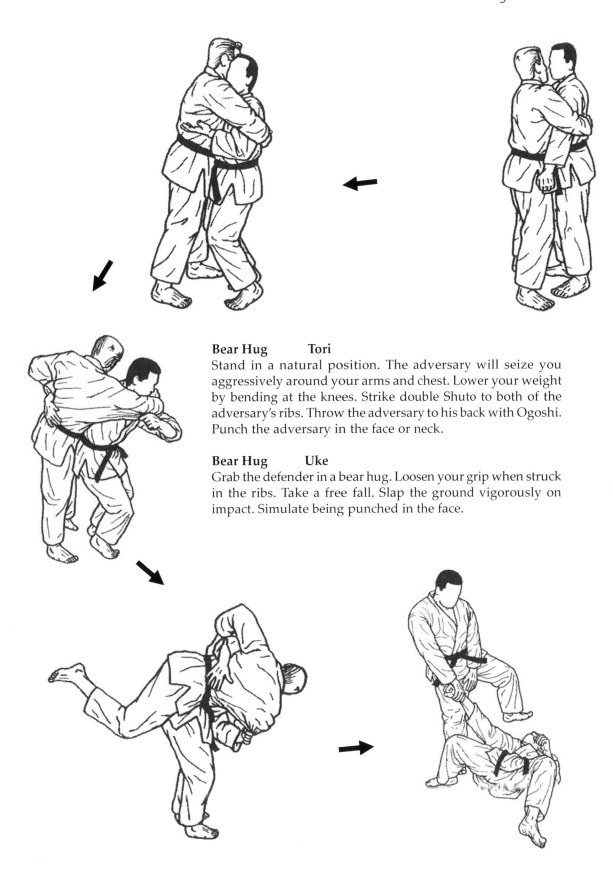

Bear Hug   Tori
Stand in a natural position. The adversary will seize you aggressively around your arms and chest. Lower your weight by bending at the knees. Strike double Shuto to both of the adversary's ribs. Throw the adversary to his back with Ogoshi. Punch the adversary in the face or neck.

Bear Hug   Uke
Grab the defender in a bear hug. Loosen your grip when struck in the ribs. Take a free fall. Slap the ground vigorously on impact. Simulate being punched in the face.

4th Kyu Green Belt

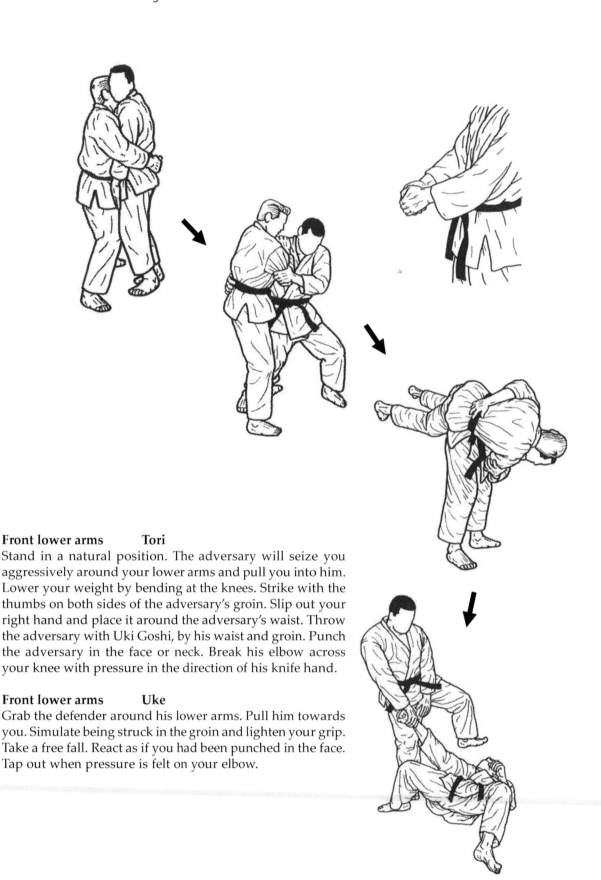

Front lower arms   Tori
Stand in a natural position. The adversary will seize you aggressively around your lower arms and pull you into him. Lower your weight by bending at the knees. Strike with the thumbs on both sides of the adversary's groin. Slip out your right hand and place it around the adversary's waist. Throw the adversary with Uki Goshi, by his waist and groin. Punch the adversary in the face or neck. Break his elbow across your knee with pressure in the direction of his knife hand.

Front lower arms   Uke
Grab the defender around his lower arms. Pull him towards you. Simulate being struck in the groin and lighten your grip. Take a free fall. React as if you had been punched in the face. Tap out when pressure is felt on your elbow.

Question 9 - Mugs

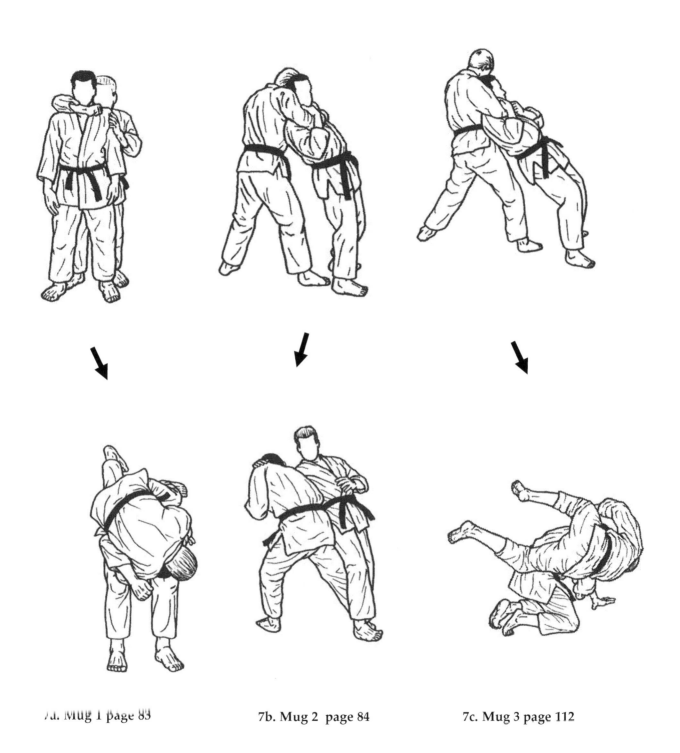

7a. Mug 1 page 83   7b. Mug 2 page 84   7c. Mug 3 page 112

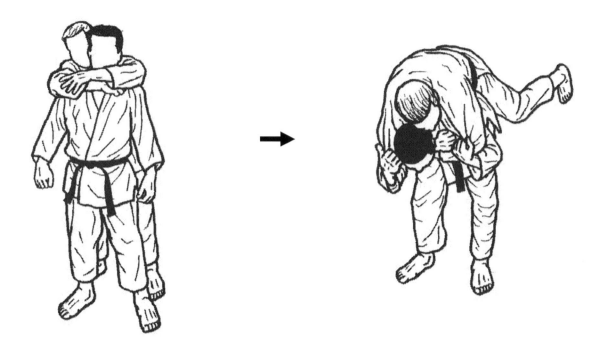

Mug 4 Tori

Stand in a natural position. The adversary will attack you wildly, both arms around your neck. Reach up, and grab both of his arms. Tuck your chin in and lower your center of gravity by bending at the knees. Bend forward at the waist and flip the adversary to his back. Follow up with a stomp to the adversary's head. Look for the next aggressor. Kiai loudly throughout the technique.

Mug 4 Uke

Grab the adversary with both arms around the neck. Kiai loudly. You will somersault over his back. Land on the balls of your feet and your shoulder blades. Exhale sharply and do not let your back touch the ground on impact.

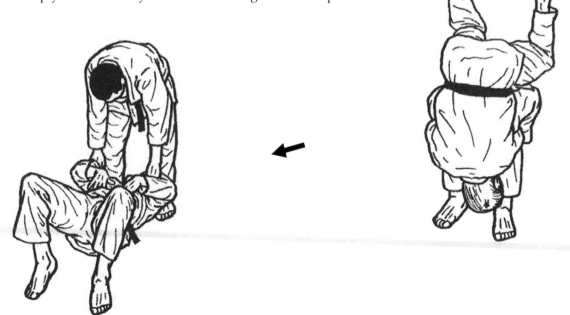

Multiple attack   Tori

The first adversary attacks with a right stomach thrust. Execute Taisabaki 5. As you turn you will notice the second adversary. Throw the first adversary with Kotegaeshi into the path of the second. Hold your ground so that the second adversary must come around his injured accomplice. As he attacks with a face slap, throw him to his back with Ippon Seionage.

Multiple attack   Uke 1

Attack the defender with a right stomach thrust. As you feel the Kansetsuwaza on your elbow take a large step around with your left leg. You will then be thrown with Kotegaeshi.

Multiple attack   Uke 2

As soon as your partner attacks, try and attack with a face slap to the side of the defender's head. Step back as your accomplice is drawn into your path. Step around your fallen accomplice and attack the defender with a face slap.

4th Kyu Green Belt

Question 10 - Multiple Attack

Question 11 - Knife Attacks

11a. Knife Thrust to Stomach page 85

11b. Face Slash page 86

11c. Carotid Stab page 114

4th Kyu Green Belt

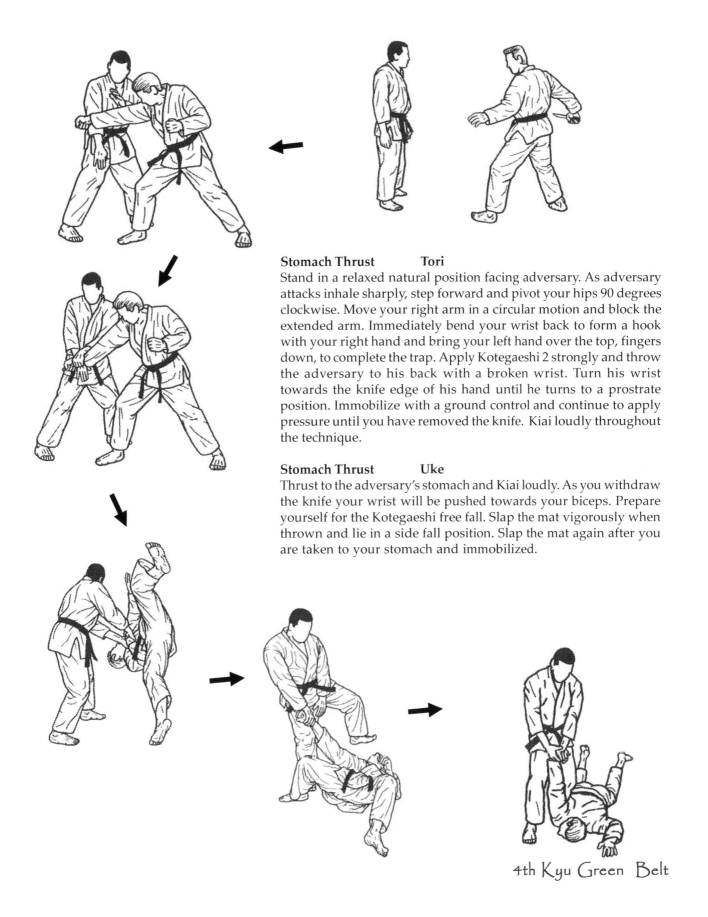

Stomach Thrust   Tori

Stand in a relaxed natural position facing adversary. As adversary attacks inhale sharply, step forward and pivot your hips 90 degrees clockwise. Move your right arm in a circular motion and block the extended arm. Immediately bend your wrist back to form a hook with your right hand and bring your left hand over the top, fingers down, to complete the trap. Apply Kotegaeshi 2 strongly and throw the adversary to his back with a broken wrist. Turn his wrist towards the knife edge of his hand until he turns to a prostrate position. Immobilize with a ground control and continue to apply pressure until you have removed the knife. Kiai loudly throughout the technique.

Stomach Thrust   Uke

Thrust to the adversary's stomach and Kiai loudly. As you withdraw the knife your wrist will be pushed towards your biceps. Prepare yourself for the Kotegaeshi free fall. Slap the mat vigorously when thrown and lie in a side fall position. Slap the mat again after you are taken to your stomach and immobilized.

4th Kyu Green Belt

Knife Face slash   Tori

As adversary attacks with a face slash, step forward into left front stance. Inhale sharply and execute left Kote strike to the adversary's lower forearm. Chamber your right hand making a tight fist. Step in, yell loudly and strike with your right forearm to the side of the adversary's neck. Execute Haraigoshi. Strike the adversary on the ground with a foot stomp. Brace his right elbow against your knee and shin. Take the weapon with your right hand. Kiai throughout the technique.

Face Slash   Uke

Step forward with your right foot. Execute a right face slash with a knife to the adversary's left cheek. Exhale sharply, yelling as you strike. Exhale as you are struck. Execute a side fall. Remember to exhale and slap the ground vigorously. Slap the ground again as you feel pressure against your elbow

4th Kyu Green Belt

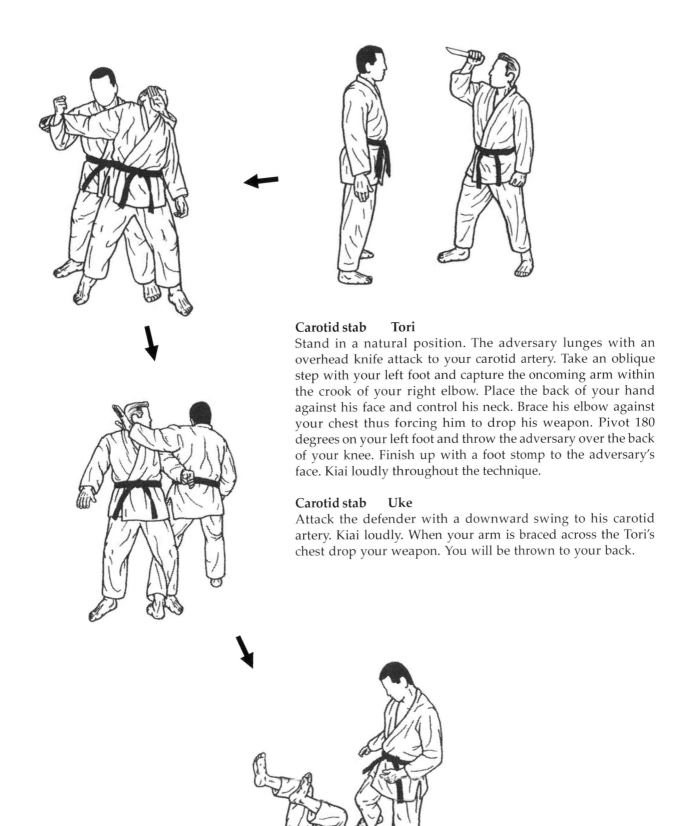

Carotid stab   Tori

Stand in a natural position. The adversary lunges with an overhead knife attack to your carotid artery. Take an oblique step with your left foot and capture the oncoming arm within the crook of your right elbow. Place the back of your hand against his face and control his neck. Brace his elbow against your chest thus forcing him to drop his weapon. Pivot 180 degrees on your left foot and throw the adversary over the back of your knee. Finish up with a foot stomp to the adversary's face. Kiai loudly throughout the technique.

Carotid stab   Uke

Attack the defender with a downward swing to his carotid artery. Kiai loudly. When your arm is braced across the Tori's chest drop your weapon. You will be thrown to your back.

4th Kyu Green Belt

Question 12 - Club Attacks

12a. Club Strike to Side of Head page 87

12b. Club to the Top of the Head page 115

12c. Club Backhand to Head page 116

4th Kyu Green Belt

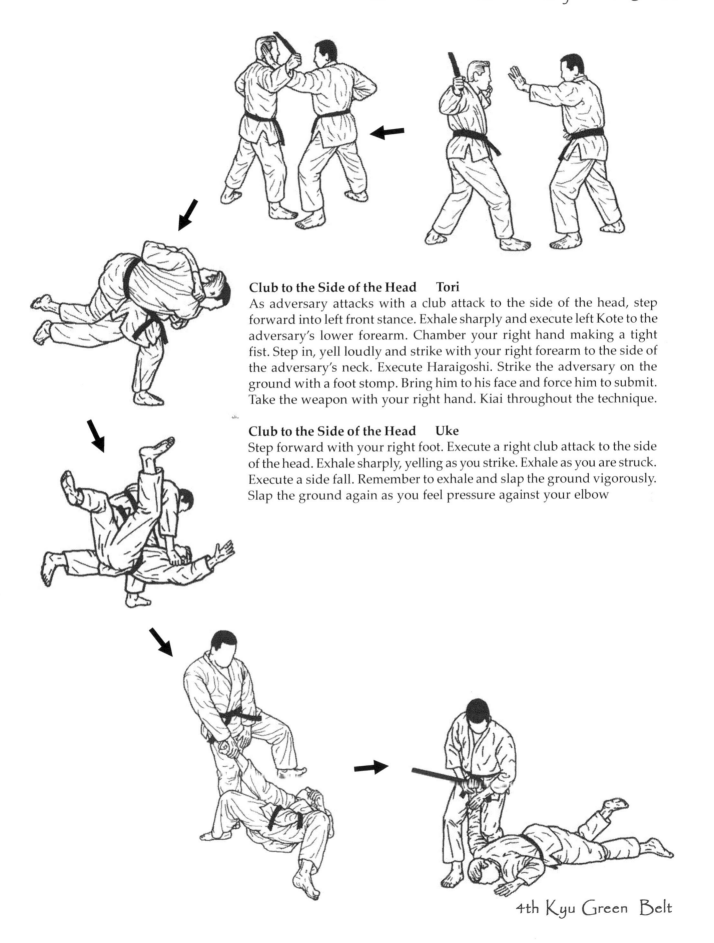

Club to the Side of the Head   Tori

As adversary attacks with a club attack to the side of the head, step forward into left front stance. Exhale sharply and execute left Kote to the adversary's lower forearm. Chamber your right hand making a tight fist. Step in, yell loudly and strike with your right forearm to the side of the adversary's neck. Execute Haraigoshi. Strike the adversary on the ground with a foot stomp. Bring him to his face and force him to submit. Take the weapon with your right hand. Kiai throughout the technique.

Club to the Side of the Head   Uke

Step forward with your right foot. Execute a right club attack to the side of the head. Exhale sharply, yelling as you strike. Exhale as you are struck. Execute a side fall. Remember to exhale and slap the ground vigorously. Slap the ground again as you feel pressure against your elbow

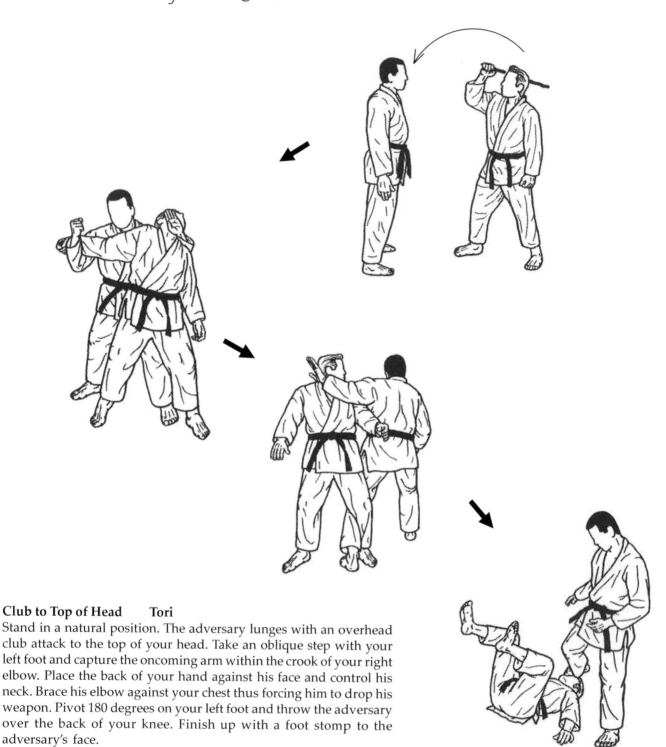

Club to Top of Head   Tori

Stand in a natural position. The adversary lunges with an overhead club attack to the top of your head. Take an oblique step with your left foot and capture the oncoming arm within the crook of your right elbow. Place the back of your hand against his face and control his neck. Brace his elbow against your chest thus forcing him to drop his weapon. Pivot 180 degrees on your left foot and throw the adversary over the back of your knee. Finish up with a foot stomp to the adversary's face.

Club to Top of Head   Uke

Attack the defender with a downward swing to the top of his head. When your elbow is braced across the defender's chest, drop your weapon. You will be thrown to your back.

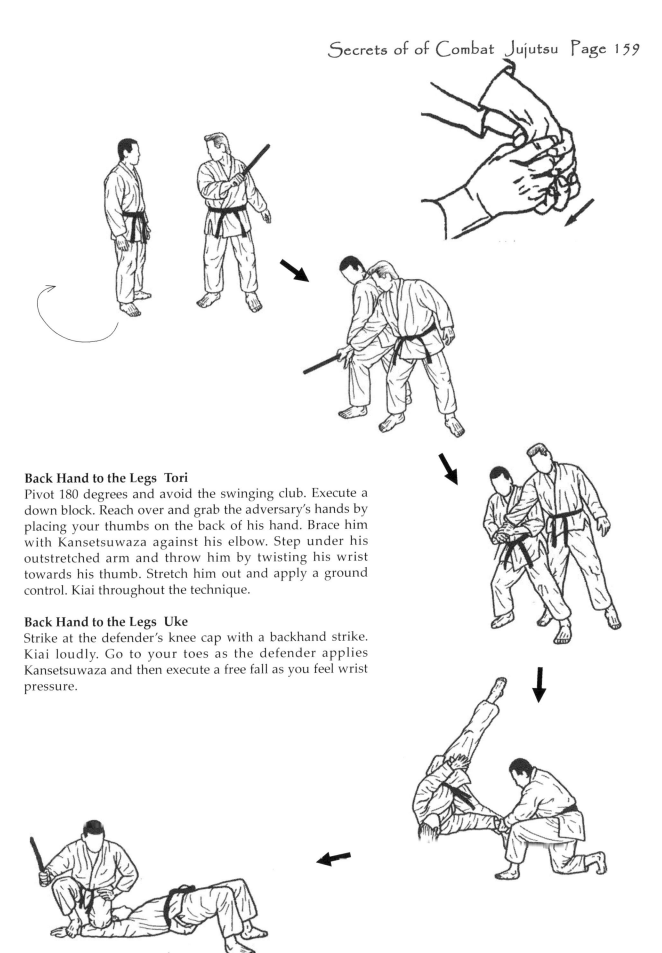

Back Hand to the Legs Tori

Pivot 180 degrees and avoid the swinging club. Execute a down block. Reach over and grab the adversary's hands by placing your thumbs on the back of his hand. Brace him with Kansetsuwaza against his elbow. Step under his outstretched arm and throw him by twisting his wrist towards his thumb. Stretch him out and apply a ground control. Kiai throughout the technique.

Back Hand to the Legs Uke

Strike at the defender's knee cap with a backhand strike. Kiai loudly. Go to your toes as the defender applies Kansetsuwaza and then execute a free fall as you feel wrist pressure.

4th Kyu Green Belt

Question 13 - Front Chokes

Double Front Choke Kansetsuwaza   Tori
Stand in a relaxed natural position. The adversary will choke you with both hands. Bring your left hand up and trap his right hand. Strike Seiken to a vital point on the adversary's face. Step in left foot and apply Kansetsuwaza to the adversary's elbow. Bring him to the ground strongly and immobilize him with your ground control. Kiai throughout the technique.

Double Front Choke Kansetsuwaza   Uke
Grab the defender's with both hands around his neck. Kiai loudly. Move your head back to simulate being struck. As your elbow is locked, bend forward slightly. Slap the side of your body as you feel pressure on your elbow. You will be fully unbalanced at this point and unable to step. Fall forward turning your head away from the captured arm. This will alleviate the pressure. Slap the mat vigorously when you feel pressure on your shoulder.

Single Hand Choke Kotegaeshi   **Tori**

Stand in a relaxed natural position. The adversary will grab your throat with his right hand. Turn your left hand up, palm facing towards you and grab the back of his right hand. Simultaneously strike to the side of his head. Step down and apply Kotegaeshi 3. Strike the adversary with Fomi Komi Geri to the temple. Twist the adversary's wrist towards the knife edge of his hand until he turns to his face. Immobilize him by locking his arm with Kansetsuwaza. Kiai throughout the technique.

Sngle Hand Choke Kotegaeshi   **Uke**

Grab the defender's throat with your right hand. Kiai loudly. When you are slapped in the head relax your grip. Simulate being struck and allow the Tori to turn your wrist. Execute a free fall. Relax and go with the wrist turning action. Slap when you feel pressure on your shoulder.

Question 14 - Formal Throws

14a. Ippon Seionage page 90   14b. Koshi Guruma page 91   14c. Uki Otoshi page 92

14d. Osotogari page 118   14e. Sukuinage page 119

4th Kyu Green Belt

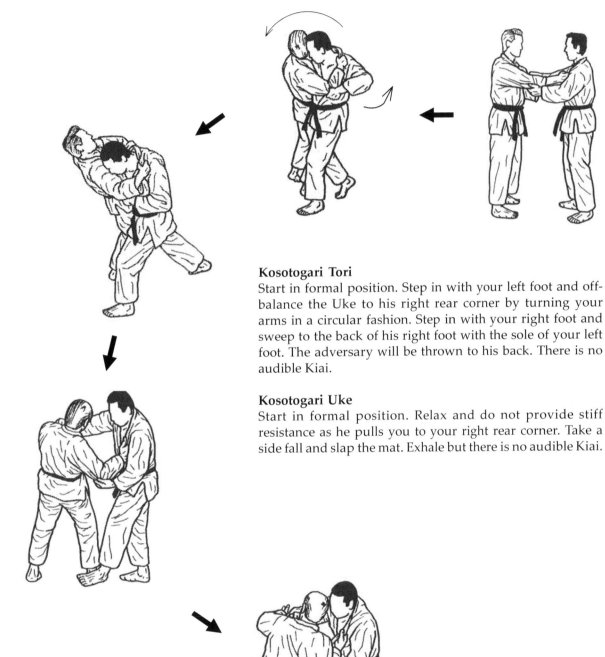

Kosotogari Tori
Start in formal position. Step in with your left foot and off-balance the Uke to his right rear corner by turning your arms in a circular fashion. Step in with your right foot and sweep to the back of his right foot with the sole of your left foot. The adversary will be thrown to his back. There is no audible Kiai.

Kosotogari Uke
Start in formal position. Relax and do not provide stiff resistance as he pulls you to your right rear corner. Take a side fall and slap the mat. Exhale but there is no audible Kiai.

4th Kyu Green Belt

Ogoshi Tori

Grab the Uke formally on his right side. Step diagonally across with your right foot inside of his feet. Pull the Uke's right arm at the elbow and unbalance him to his right front corner. Reach around and grab the Uke's waist. Pivot on your right foot, bringing your left foot in parallel to your right. Your waist should be lower than your adversary's waist. Bend at the waist draping the adversary onto your back. Pull him down to your left and look left so he rolls over your hip and not your head. There is no audible Kiai.

Ogoshi Uke

Start in formal position. Relax and do not provide stiff resistance as he pulls you to your right front corner. Roll over his hip and take a side fall and slap the mat. Exhale but there is no audible Kiai.

Uki Goshi Tori
Grab the Uke formally on his right side. Step diagonally across with your right foot inside of his feet. Pull the Uke's right arm at the elbow and unbalance him to his right front corner. Reach around and grab the Uke's waist. Step in with your left foot bringing it behind your right foot. Bring your hip in to the Uke's groin area below his waist. Lift the opponent onto the side of your hip dropping him 90 degrees to your body.

Uki Goshi Uke
Start in formal position. Relax and do not provide stiff resistance as he pulls you to your right front corner. Roll over his hip and take a side fall and slap the mat. Exhale but there is no audible Kiai.

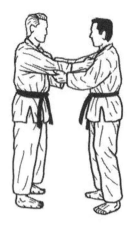

Ju-jutsu Taiotoshi Tori

Start in a formal position. Step diagonally across with your right foot. Pull the adversary's right arm at the elbow. This action will unbalance him to his right front corner. Step in with your left foot behind your right foot outside your Uke's left foot. Pivot onto your left knee and extend your right foot blocking his right ankle. You should be on the ball of your foot with your heel pointing upward. Your knee should be pointing downwards to avoid dislocation should the adversary fall on your knee. Turn your head away from the adversary as you push and pull your arms as if using a bow and arrow. Straighten your right leg under your opponent's knee causing him to go up on his toes and fall forward.

Ju-jutsu Taiotoshi Uke

Start in formal position. Relax and do not provide stiff resistance as he pulls you to your right front corner. Trip over his extended leg. Take a side fall and slap the mat. Exhale but there is no audible Kiai.

4th Kyu Green Belt

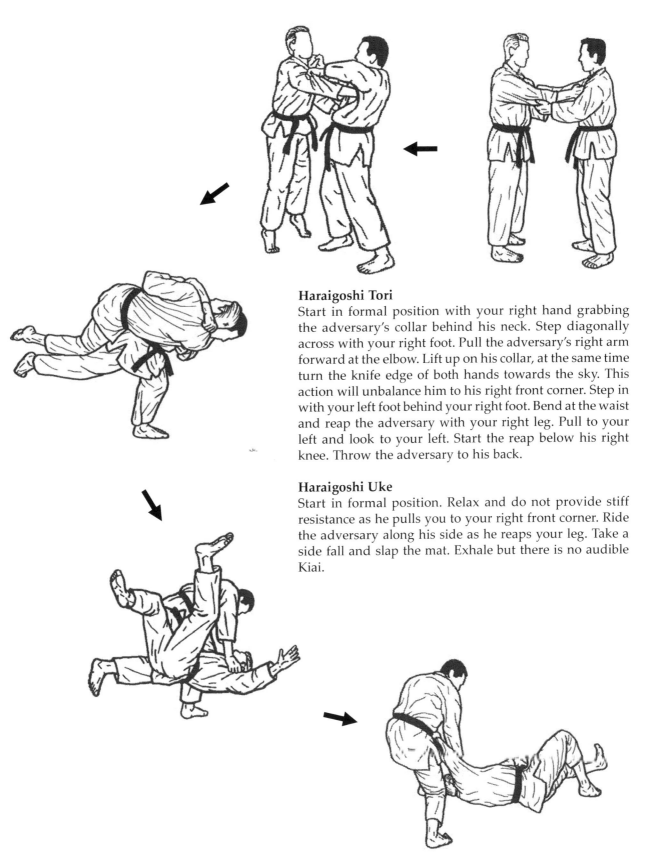

Haraigoshi Tori
Start in formal position with your right hand grabbing the adversary's collar behind his neck. Step diagonally across with your right foot. Pull the adversary's right arm forward at the elbow. Lift up on his collar, at the same time turn the knife edge of both hands towards the sky. This action will unbalance him to his right front corner. Step in with your left foot behind your right foot. Bend at the waist and reap the adversary with your right leg. Pull to your left and look to your left. Start the reap below his right knee. Throw the adversary to his back.

Haraigoshi Uke
Start in formal position. Relax and do not provide stiff resistance as he pulls you to your right front corner. Ride the adversary along his side as he reaps your leg. Take a side fall and slap the mat. Exhale but there is no audible Kiai.

4th Kyu Green Belt

Sonota Waza (Unofficial Techniques Taught At 4th Kyu)

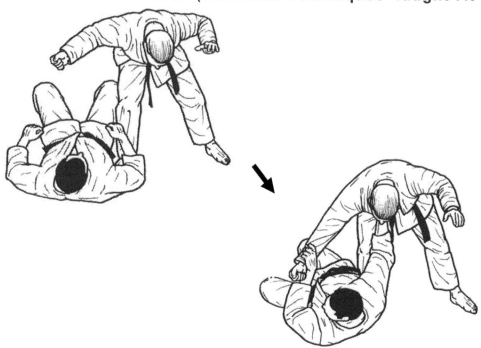

Ground Punch Tori

You are lying on your back right knee up. The adversary attacks from your right side with a hooking punch. Sit up and block his right forearm with your left hand. Strike with right Koko to his jaw. Rotate your hips 180 degrees and throw him over your body. Continue to turn and straddle his chest finishing him with Kansetsuwaza.

Ground Punch Uke

Attack the defender with a hooking punch as he is lying on the ground. Take a rolling side fall over his body. Slap the mat to indicate submission when you feel pressure on the elbow.

4th Kyu Green Belt

Lunge Punch Hair Pull   Tori
The adversary attempts to punch you in the face with a lunge punch. Step to the side as in Taisabaki 4. Grab his hair deep at the roots. Pull backwards and stomp kick him in the knee. Pull him to the ground and stomp kick him in the head.

Lunge Punch Hair Pull   Uke
Strike at the defender's face with a right lunge punch. You will be thrown violently to your back.

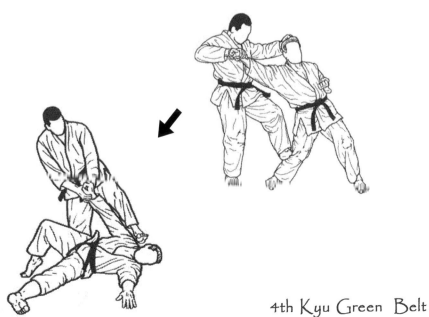

Lunge Punch Irimi Nage   Tori

The adversary attempts to punch you in the face with a lunge punch. Step to the side as in Taisabaki 4. Drive his head down forward by grabbing him at the collar. Change directions as he resists your push and bring the right arm up and throw him with Irimi Nage. Kiai throughout the technique.

Lunge Punch Irimi Nage   Uke

Punch the defender in his face with a right lunge punch. Kiai loudly. Go with the defender as he pushes you forward , but try to straighten back up so as not to fall forward. Fall to your back with   the Irimi Nage throw.

Hooking Punch Throat Throw Back   Tori

Stand in a natural position. The adversary lunges with a hooking punch to your face. Attack his hand with a left Kote. Push his left shoulder with your right hand causing him to turn. Place the back of your hand against his face and control his neck. Brace his elbow against your chest. Pivot 180 degrees on your left foot and throw the adversary over the back of your knee. Finish up with a foot stomp to the adversary's face.

Hooking Punch Throat Throw Back   Uke

Attack the defender with a hooking punch. When your elbow is braced across the defender's chest, slap to indicate submission. You will be thrown to your back.

4th Kyu Green Belt

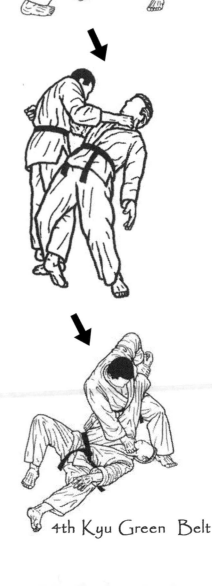

Tiger Claw Jime   Tori
From a kneeling formal position grab the Uke's lapel with
your left hand. Reach in and grab him by the trachea.
Your fingers should press into his throat and there should
be no space between your palm and his throat. Squeeze
until he submits.

Tiger Claw Jime   Uke
Assume a kneeling formal position facing the Tori. Slap
the side of your body when you feel pressure from the
choke.

For illustrative purposes a defense against a punch with
an Osotogari follow up is shown.

4th Kyu Green Belt

Scissors Hadaka Jime   Tori
Avoid a thrusting left punch. Strike to the adversary's kidneys with a right punch. Step in with your left leg and wrap your left arm around the defender's neck and control his head with the back of your hand. Violently bring your right hand behind his neck. Scissor the adversary's neck between your forearms. Bring him to the ground immediately and continue to apply the strangle.

Scissors Hadaka Jime   Uke
Strike to the adversary's face with a left lunge punch. Slap the side of your body when you feel pressure from the strangle hold.

4th Kyu Green Belt

Kata Ha Jime   Tori
Come directly behind the Uke who is in a kneeling postion. Drop to your left knee. Raise his rght hand by bringing your right hand under his arm. Reach across his throat with your left arm and grab his collar with your left hand. Bring your right hand behind his head. Immediately squeeze and strangle him, while pulling his head to your left until he submits.

Kata Ha Jime   Uke
Assume a kneeling formal position. Slap the side of your body when you feel pressure from the choke.

For illustrative purposes a defense against a lunge punch with a standing Kata Ha Jime is shown.

Belt Tests and Promotion Requirements

6th Kyu Orange

Time-in-grade: 20 lessons

1. Formal Bow and Ukemi
Vol 1: Page 58 - 61
a. Three sitting, squatting, standing b. Side falls (one hand, two hands)
c. Rolls (both sides)

2. Taisabaki
Vol 1: Page 62- 69
(Without Uke)
a. Formal b. Escape c. Punishment

3. Kotegaeshi
Vol 1: Page 70 - 72
a. 1 through 3 on either side

4. Kansetsuwaza
Vol 1: Page 73
a. Left or right

5. Wrist Grabs
Vol 1: Page 74 -77
a. Double wrist (Kansetsuwaza or Kotegaeshi) b. Single wrist (Kansetsuwaza or Kotegaeshi)

6. Lapel Grabs
Vol 1: Page 78 - 81
a. One single hand grab (Kansetsuwaza or Kotegaeshi) b. One double hand grab (Kansetsuwaza or Kotegaeshi)

7. Body Grabs from Behind
Vol 1: Page 82
a. Upper chest grab (Seionage)

8. Mugs
Vol 1: Page 83- 84
a. Around the neck b. Around the neck, one step back

9. Weapons Attacks
Vol 1: Page 85 - 87
a. Knife thrust to stomach (Kotegaeshi) b. Face slash (Ippon Seionage) c. Club to the side of the head (Ippon Seionage)

10. Formal Moves
Vol 1: Page 90 -92
a. Ippon Seoi nage b. Koshi-guruma c. Uki Otoshi

5th Kyu Yellow

Time-in-grade: 20 lessons

1. Formal Bow and Ukemi
Vol 1: Page 58 - 61
a. Three sitting, squatting, standing b. Side falls (one hand, two hands)
c. Rolls (both sides)
Vol 1: Page 97
d. One man obstacle (right and left)

2. Taisabaki
Vol 1: Page 62- 69
(Without Uke)
a. Formal b. Escape c. Punishment

3. Kotegaeshi
Vol 1: Page 70 - 72
a. 1 through 3, right and left
Vol 1: Page 100
b. Kotegaeshi 4

4. Kansetsuwaza
Vol 1: Page 73
a. Left or right

5. Wrist Grabs
Vol 1: Page 74 - 81
a. Double wrist (Kansetsuwaza or Kotegaeshi) b. Single wrist (Kansetsuwaza or Kotegaeshi)
Vol 1: Page 102-104
c. Cross wrist (Kansetsuwaza or Kotegaeshi) d. Double hand on one wrist (Shuto strike)

6. Lapel Grabs
Vol 1: Page 78 -71
a. One single hand grab (Kansetsuwaza or Kotegaeshi)
b. One double hand grab (Kansetsuwaza or Kotegaeshi)

Vol 1: Page 106 - 107
c. Single pull close (right and left sides) I.Osotogari II.Ude-garami

7. Body Grabs from Behind
Vol 1: Page 82
a. Upper chest grab (Seionage)
Vol 1: Page 109 - 110
b. Lower arms (Sukuinage) c. Under arms (Kansetsuwaza)

8. Mugs
Vol 1: Page 83- 84
a. Around the neck b. Around the neck, one step back
Vol 1: Page 112
b. Around the neck, one step back c. Around the neck full unbalance

9. Weapons Attacks
Vol 1: Page 85 - 86
a. Knife thrust to stomach (Kotegaeshi) b. Face slash (Ippon Seionage)
Vol 1: Page 114
c. Carotid stab (Kotegaeshi)
Vol 1: Page 87
d. Club to the side of the head (Ippon Seionage)
Vol 1: Page 115 - 116
e. Club to the top of the head (Kotegaeshi) f. Backhand to the side of the head (Kansetsuwaza)

10. Formal Moves
Vol 1: Page 90 -92
a. Ippon Seoi nage b. Koshi-guruma c. Uki Otoshi
Vol 1: Page 118- 119
d. Osotogari e. Sukuinage

4th Kyu Green

Time-in-grade: 32 lessons

1. Formal Bow and Ukemi
Vol 1: Page 58 -61
a. Three sitting, squatting, standing b. Side falls (one hand, two hands) c. Rolls (both sides)
Vol 1: Page 126 - 127
c. Forward somersault (with and without hands)
d. Two man obstacle (right and left)

2. Taisabaki
Vol 1: Pages 62 -69
a. Full action
Vol 1: Page 129
b. Question:What is Atemiwaza? c. Question: Name four hand techniques used in Atemiwaza? (Seiken, Uraken, Shuto, Haito)

3. Kotegaeshi (Right & Left)
Vol 1: Page 70 -72
a. 1 through 3
Vol 1: Page 100
b. 4
Vol 1: Page 131
c. 5

4. Kansetsuwaza
Vol 1: Page 76
a. Single wrist
Vol 1: Page 132
b. Elbow
Vol 1: Page 133
c. Shoulder

5. Wrist Grabs
Vol 1: Page 74 - 77
a. Double wrist (Kansetsuwaza and Kotegaeshi) b. Single wrist (Kansetsuwaza and Kotegaeshi)
Vol 1: Page 102, 103
c. Cross wrist (Kansetsuwaza and Kotegaeshi)
Vol 1: Page 104, 135
d. Double hand on one wrist (Shuto strike, Irimi Nage)

6. Lapel Grabs
Vol 1: Page 137, 138
a. Single hand grab with throws (Ippon Seionage, Haraigoshi)
Vol 1: Page 78, 79
b. Double hand grab (Kotegaeshi 3, Kansetsuwaza)
Vol 1: Page 139, 140
c. Single hand cross lapel (Kansetsuwaza)
Vol 1: Page 106 - 107
d. Single pull close (right and left sides) I.Osotogari II.Ude-garami

7. Body Grabs from Behind
Vol 1: Page 82
a. Upper chest grab (Seionage)
Vol 1: Page 109
b. Lower arms (Sukuinage)
Vol 1: Page 110, 142
c. Under arms (Ankle pull, double ankle pull)

8. Front Body Grabs
Vol 1: Page 143 - 146
a. Front neck embrace (Osotogari) b. Chest embrace (Koshi Guruma) c. Bear hug (Ogoshi) d. Lower arms (Uki Goshi)

9. Mugs
Vol 1: Page 83, 84

a. Around the neck b. Around the neck, one step back
Vol 1: Page 112
c. Around the neck full unbalance
Vol 1: Page 148
d. Flying mare

10. Multiple Attack
Vol 1 Page: 150 -151
a. Defend from a two man attack with knife and club in rapid order (Kotegaeshi, Ippon Seionage)

11. Knife Attacks
Vol 1 Page: 85
a. Knife thrust to stomach (Kotegaeshi)
Vol 1 Page: 153 (deflection)
Vol 1: Page 86
b. Face slash (Ippon Seionage)
Vol 1: Page 154 (Harai Goshi)
Vol 1: Page 114
c. Carotid stab (Kotegaesh)
Vol 1: Page 155 (Throat throwback)

12. Club Attacks
Vol 1: Page 87
a. Club to the side of the head (Koshi Guruma)
Vol 1: Page 157 (Haraioshi)
Vol 1: Page 115
b. Club to the top of the head (Kotegaeshi)
Vol 1: Page 158 (Throat throwback)
Vol 1: Page 116
c. Backhand to the side of the head (Ude gatame)

d. Backhand to the legs
Vol 1: Page 159
(Gyaku Kotegaeshi)

13. Front Chokes
Vol 1: Page 160
a. Two hands on the neck
(Kansetsuwaza)
Vol 1: Page 161
b. One hand on the neck
(Kotegaeshi 3)

14. Formal Moves
Vol 1: Page 90 - 92
a. Ippon Seionage b. Koshi
Guruma c Uki otoshi.
Vol 1: Page 118, 119
 d. Osotogari e. Sukuinage
Vol 1: Page 163 -167
f.Kosotogari. g. Ogoshi h. Uki
Goshi i. Jujutsu Taiotoshi j.
Harai Goshi

3rd Kyu Brown

Time-in-grade: 6 months

1. Formal Bow and Ukemi
a. What is the meaning of Ukemi?
Vol 1: Page 58-61
b. Demonstrate Ukemi:
1. Three sitting, squatting, standing 2. Side falls (one hand, two hands) 4. Rolls (left/right)
Vol 1: Page 126
5. Forward Somersault (with and without hands)
Vol 2: Page 42- 46
5. Backrolls, ([left/right) 6. Dead front fall 7. Side seperation (left/right) 8. Free fall roll 9. Kotegaeshi rolls, (left/right) 10. 3 man obstacle

2. Taisabaki
Vol 1: Page 62 -69
a. What is the meaning of Taisabaki? b. Can you switch from one to another? c. Formal d. Escape e. Punishment (Seiken)
Vol 2: page 48 - 67
f. Uraken g. Preparation kicks h. With throws.

3. Kotegaeshi
a. What is the meaning of Kotegaeshi?
Vol 1: Page 70 -72
b. 1 through 3 (right and left)
Vol 1: Page 100
c. 4 (right and left)
Vol 1: Page 131
d. 5 (right and left)
Vol 2: Page 69
e. 6 (right and left

4. Kansetsuwaza
a. What is the meaning of Kansetsuwaza?
b. Demonstrate Kansetsuwaza (left/right):
Vol 1: Page 73
1. Basic stepping in - stepping back
Vol 2: Page 71 - 75
2. Stepping in - stepping in 3. Stepping in - stepping in to produce wrist punishment 4.Stepping in, stepping back to produce wrist punishment 5. Double wrist grab 6. Double elbow grab.

5. Wrist Grabs and pendulums
Vol 2: Page 76 -84
:a. Four double b. Four single, same side c. four cross wrist d. Three double hand on one wrist e. Pendulum to the rear and to the front.

6. Lapel Grabs
Vol 2: Page 85 - 92
a. Three double with out-twisted hands b. Three double stiff armed c. Two lapel bent arm pull close (left and right) d. One cross lapel, pull around (left and right)

7. Front Body Grabs
Vol 1: Page 143 -146
a. Front neck embrace (Osotogari) b. Chest embrace (Koshi Guruma) c. Bear Hug (Ogoshi) d. Lower arms (Uki-goshi)

8. Body Grabs from Behind
Vol 2: Page 94 - 96
a. Two upper arms b. Two lower arms c. Two under arms

9. Mugs
Vol 1: Page 83, 84
1 a. Around the neck b. Around the neck, one step back
Vol 1: Page 112
c. Around the neck full unbalance
Vol 1: Page 148
d. Flying mare
Vol 2: 98, 99
e. Knee in back.
2 Resisting mug

10. Chokes
Vol 1: Page 160, 161
a. Two from the front
Vol 2: Page 101-104
b. Two from the side c. Two from the rear

11. Rapid Order Attack
Vol 2: Page 105
From mug #1, same man attacks with a hooking right hand after having been thrown.

12. Multiple Attack
Vol 2: Page 106, 107
Three man attack (knife, club, punch)

13. Knife Attacks
Vol 2: Page 108 - 114
a. Three knife thrust to stomach b. Three face slashes c. Three carotid stabs d. One looping right body slash e. One backhand to the face f. One throat thrust

14. Club Attacks
Vol 2: Page 115 - 117
a. Three club to the left side of the head b. One club to the right side of the head with the left hand. c. Two to the top of the head d. One to the shins, backhand e. One backhand to the head.

15. Aid Someone Being Attacked
Vol 2: Page 118-119
a. Knife thrust to stomach b. Stick to the side of the head

16. Formal Moves
Vol 1: Page 90 -92
1. Ippon Seoi nage 2. Koshi-guruma 3 Uki otoshi.
Vol 1: Page 118, 119
4. Osotogari 5. Sukuinage
Vol 1: Page 163 - 167
6. Kosotogari. 7. Ogoshi 8. Uki-goshi 9. Jujutsu Tai otoshi 10. Harai-goshi
Vol 2: Page 121- 126
11. Judo Tai otoshi 12. Yama arashi (2 ways) 13. Ouchigari 14. Kouchi-gari 15. Morote Seoi nage 16. Tomoe nage.

2nd Kyu Brown

Time-in-grade: 6 months

1.1. Formal Bow and Ukemi
a. What is the meaning of Ukemi?
Vol 1: Page 58-61
b. Demonstrate Ukemi:
1. Three sitting, squatting, standing 2. Side falls (one hand, two hands) 4. Rolls (left/right)
Vol 1: Page 126
5. Forward Somersault (with and without hands)
Vol 2: Page 42- 46
5. Backrolls, ([left/right) 6. Dead front fall 7. Side seperation (left/right) 8. Free fall roll 9. Kotegaeshi rolls, (left /right)
Vol 2: Page 138
10. Three man obstacle

2. Taisabaki
Vol 1: Page 62 -69
a. What is the meaning of Taisabaki? b. Can you switch from one to another? c. Formal d. Escape e. Punishment (Seiken)
Vol 2: page 48 - 67
f. Uraken g. Preparation kicks h. With throws.
Vol 2: Page 140 - 156
i. To the rear j. To the rear with throws.

3. Kotegaeshi
a. What is the meaning of Kotegaeshi?
Vol 1: Page 70 -72
b. 1 through 3 (right and left)
Vol 1: Page 100
c. 4 (right and left)
Vol 1: Page 131

d. 5 (right and left)
Vol 2: Page 69
e. 6 (right and left)
Vol 2: Page 83, 84
Pendulums
f. Pendulum to the front and side (right & left)
g. Pendulum to the rear (right & left)
Vol 2: Page 159, 160
h. Kotegaeshi 7, 8

4. Kansetsu waza from formal
Vol 1: Page 73, Vol 2: 71 -73
a. Basic, stepping in, stepping back b. Stepping in, stepping in c. Stepping in, stepping in to produce wrist punishment d. Stepping in, stepping back to produce wrist punishment.

5. Devils Handshake & Tigerlock
Vol 2: Page 162- 164
a. Demonstrate Devil's Handshake (with and without clothes) from a looping punch to the head and ending with a throw.
b. Demonstrate Tigerlock (with & without clothes) from a looping punch to the head and ending with a throw.

6. Wrist Grabs
Vol 1: Page 74 - 77, Vol 2: Page 77 - 82
a. Four single on the right wrist
b. Four single on the left wrist,
c. Four single cross wrist, left or right
Vol 1: Page 102 - 104
Vol 2: Page 166

d. Four double cross wrist grabs, left or right

7. Come Alongs
Vol 2: Page 167, 168
a. 3 simple b. 3 bonelocks

8. Lapel Grabs
Vol 2: page 169 - 170
a. Three double b. Three single
c. Three double pull close

9. Body Grabs from Behind
a. Two upper arms b. Two lower arms c. Two under arms

10. Front Body Grabs
Vol 1: Page 143 -146
Vol 1: Pages 173 -176
a. Front neck embrace (Osotogari, Ogoshi) b. Chest embrace (Harai goshi, Ukigoshi) c.Lower arms (Uki-goshi, Ogoshi) d. Under arms (Koshi-guruma)

11. Mugs
Vol 1: Page 83, 84
1 a. Around the neck b. Around the neck, one step back
Vol 1: Page 112
c. Around the neck full unbalance
Vol1: Page 148
d. Flying mare
Vol 2: Page 98, 99
e. Knee in back
Vol 2: Page 178 - 181
2. (Right side only) a. Hand over mouth pull back b. Hair pull c. Full unbalance (Ouchi, Kouchi)

12. Pressure points
Vol 2: Page 182 - 183

Articulate and point out pressure points on both sides of the body (front and back)

13. Multiple Attack
Vol 2: Page 184 - 185
a. Simulate (with speed) a defense from a 4 man unarmed attack.

14. Multiple Attack
Vol 2: Page 186 - 187
a. Simulate (with speed) a defense from a 4 man attack who have a knife, a club, and 2 punches.

15. Kick Defense
Vol 2: Page 188 - 192
a. Four front kicks b. A kick to the body while lying on the stomach

16. Wall Techniques
Vol 2: Page 193 - 202
a. Two groin stabs b. Two stomach thrust c. Two carotids d. Two face slashes e. Two backhands to the face

17. Single Man Rapid Order Knife attack
Vol 2: Page 203
Uke attacks with a face slash, backhand slash, left side body slash and a stomach thrust

18. Club Attacks
Vol 2: Page 204 - 207
With speed and applying a different technique to each attack, defend from:
a. Two to the left side of the head b. Two club to the right side of the head with the left hand. c. Two to the top of the head d. One right backhand body slash e. One right backhand to the legs. f. One right hand to the legs.

19. Aid Someone Being Attacked
Vol 2: Page 208 - 209
a. A carotid knife attack b. A face slash.

20. Formal Moves
Vol 1: Page 90 -92
1. Ippon Seoi nage 2. Koshi-guruma 3 Uki otoshi.
Vol 1: Page 118, 119
4. Osotogari 5. Sukuinage
Vol 1: Page 163 - 167
6. Kosotogari. 7. Ogoshi 8. Uki-goshi 9. Jujutsu Tai otoshi 10. Harai-goshi
Vol 2: Page 121 - 126
11. Judo Tai otoshi 12. Yama arashi (2 ways) 13. Ouchigari 14. Kouchi-gari 15. Morote Seoi nage 16. Tomoe nage.
Vol 2: Page 212 -217
17. Uki waza 18. Osoto-guruma 19. Kata guruma 20. Sode tsuri komi-goshi 21. Soto Makikomi (3 ways) 22. Tsuri goshi

1st Kyu Brown Belt

Time-in-grade: 6 months

1. General knowledge
a. What is the meaning of Miyama Ryu?
b. Why that name?
c. From whom it and where did it originate?
d. What is Ukemi?
e. Tell the difference in the arts (Judo, Jujutsu, Aikido, and Karate)
f. Demonstrate all types of Ukemi (Judo, Jujutsu, and Aikido)
g. Demonstrate Ippon Seoi nage in the Judo form and then in the Jujutsu form.

2. Taisabaki
a. What is the meaning of Tai sabaki?
b. How many does Miyama use?
c. Can you switch from one to another?
d. Demonstrate all your Tai sabaki defenses.
1. Formal 2. Escape 3. Punishment (Seiken) 4. Uraken 5. Kicking 6. Cat step escapes 7. With throws 8. To the rear 9. To the rear with throws

3. Pressure points
a. Articulate and point out 21 pressure points on both sides of the body (front and back)
b. What are pressure points mainly used for?

4. Vital areas
a. Show and name 14 vital areas on the front and back of the body.
b. What are the vital areas mainly used for?
c. Under what circumstances would you strike for a vital area?

5. Atemi Waza
a. What is the meaning of Atemi waza?
b. Demonstrate Atemi to the Vital areas:

1. Four open hand strike giving Japanese names 2. Three different ways with the closed fist giving Japanese names 3. Three distinct ways with the foot 4. Name six parts of the leg used for Atemi. Name eight parts of the arm used for Atemi.

6. Come Alongs
Demonstrate six simple and six bonelocks.

7. Mugs
1. Around the neck 2. Around the neck/ one step back 3. Around the neck full unbalance 4. Flying mare 5. Knee in back 6. Hand over mouth pull back 7. Hair pull 8. Full unbalance (Ouchi, Kouchi) 9. Ouster 10. Sleeper hold 11. Full Nelson 12. Half nelson 13. Walking mug 14. Neck grab (Aiki kneeling)15. Neck grab (Goshin jutsu) 16 Neck grab (Scoop back of heel with instep 17. Front knee dislocation.

8. Body Grabs from Behind
a. Two upper arms b. Two lower arms c. Two under arms

9. Front Body Grabs
a. Front neck embrace (Osotogari, Ogoshi) b. Chest embrace (Harai goshi, Uki-goshi) c. Lower arms (Uki-goshi, Ogoshi) d. Under arms (Koshi-guruma)

10. Wrist Grabs
Demonstrate all your wrist grabs, (minimum of ten moves)

11. Kotegaeshi, Kansetsu waza and Reverses
a. One through eight (right & left) b. Enter into hammerlock four different ways c. Demonstrate Devil's Handshake with and without clothing d. Reverse Kote-gaeshi two different ways e. Reverse Tigerlock using Ogoshi f. Reverse Devil's Handshake using Uki Waza g. Reverse Hammerlock using Koshi-guruma or harai-goshi h. Reverse Kansetsuwaza using Sukuinage i. Reverse Ippon Seoi nage j. Reverse Ogoshi

12. Lapel Grabs
Demonstrate all your defenses from lapel grabs (minimum of 10 moves)
ending From a Seated Position
a. Looping right punch (with or without lapel grab) b.

Douple lapel grab, pull c.
Single lapel grab, pull d.
Double hand choke e. Rear
right forearm choke f. Knife
thrust to the chest g. Face slash
h. Backhand face slash

14. Multiple Attack
a. Defend from four men who
are unarmed. Start with your
arms pinned from the rear. b.
Defend from a 4 man attack
against attackers who have a
knife, a club, one who punches
and from a back body grab.

15. Kick Defense
a. Defend from four front kicks

16. Controls
How many controls can you
demonstrate after the attacker
has been thrown to the ground.

17. Knife attacks
1. Standing: Oblique slash to
the face, backhand to the face,
side body slash, stomach thrust
2. Lying: a. Body thrust b.
Upper body slash c. Down stab
carotid 3. Stationary: a. Knife
point held to the stomach b.
Knife to the kidneys with left
arm around the neck c. Blade
to the neck with left hand on
hair pull 4. Show all the knife
techniques that you have been
taught (Show a minimum of 10
moves)

18. Clubs
Demonstrate all your club
defenses (show a minimum of
10 moves)

19. Pistol
a. To the forehead b. To the
stomach c. To the side of the
body d. To the upper back e. To
the lower back

20. Demonstrate the last eight moves of the Miyama Ryu Gokyo moving
a. Hane-goshi b. Hane
makikomi c. Uchimata d. Hiza
guruma e. Sasae Tsurikomi
ashi f. Ushiro goshi g.
Hasamae gaeshi h. Ushiro
guruma.

Rank and Promotion Procedures

Rank in Miyama Ryu is not an entitlement; it is an acknowledgement from instructor to student. It can not be bought regardless of dojo dues paid. The Ryu establishes technical guidelines for the instructors to determine how to acknowledge the student's technical ability, effort and maturity level. These promotion requirements are guidelines for instructors, and subject to the instructor's evaluation of the student. They signify the minimum requirements, which must be met for any student to hold the particular rank. As in the Koryu (classical schools of combat) the student may request but has no right to be graded.

The Miyama Ryu uses the Kyu grading system for the Mudansha (non Black Belt ranks) include white (7th kyu), orange (6th kyu), yellow (5th Kyu), green (4th Kyu) and brown (3,2,1st Kyu) and the Menkyo ranking system for the Yudansha (Black Belt Ranks). The Menkyo ranking system was a classical ranking system for Japanese Koryu.

The Miyama Ryu uses five (5) ranks from this classical era, rather than the more modern "Dan" system.

Okuiri (Entrance to Secrets) – The first graded rank of Miyama Ryu. The bearer wears a black belt and is recognized as having practiced the basics of the system. The minimum time required to reach this level is two and a half active years in the Ryu. This rank is equivalent to the 1st and 2nd degree belts of Judo.

Mokoroku (Catalog): The bearer wears a black belt and is recognized as an experienced fighter and assistant instructor. The minimum time required to reach this level is four years after Okuiri or six and a half years in the Ryu. This rank is equivalent to 3rd and 4th degree belts of Judo.

Menkyo (License): The bearer wears a black and white belt (with black ends). He is considered a skilled technician and seasoned warrior. This is the teacher's rank and the Menkyos are addressed as Sensei (teacher). The minimum time required to reach this level is five years after Mokuroko or eleven and a half years active in the Ryu. This rank is equivalent to 5th, 6th and 7th degree of Judo. This rank can only be awarded by a Dai-Shihan.

Kaiden (Everything Passed): The bearer wears a red and white belt (with red on top). He is considered a master technician and seasoned warrior. He is also considered a seasoned teacher and capable leader within the Ryu. Kaidens are addressed as Shihan. The minimum time required to reach this level is seven years since the rank of Menkyo or eighteen and a half years active in the Ryu. This rank is equivalent to the 8th degree black belt in Judo. This rank can only be awarded by a Dai-Shihan.

Dai-Shihan (1st Shihan): These are the Headmasters of the Ryu. The bearer wears a red belt with a gold stripe running through. The original Dai-Shihans were appointed by the Shinan (Founder) to be the senior administrative ranks in the Ryu. They are the living tradition of the Ryu. Their charge from Shinan is to keep the Miyama Ryu alive. In keeping with this tradition any future Dai-Shihan will be appointed by unanimous agreement of the other Dai-Shihan. This rank is equivalent to 9th degree black belt in Judo.

The three Dai- Shihans appointed by the founder Shinan Pereira are Demetrious Milliaressis, Dr. William Duke, and D'Arcy Rahming.

Shinan: The "Founder", Antonio Pereira was the First Headmaster of the Ryu. The Shinan wore a red and black belt with red on top and gold ends. This title is a part of Miyama Ryu history and no future Miyama Ryu practitioner can hold this title. Shinan was the only 10th degree Black Belt of Miyama Ryu.

* **Soke** (Family Inheritor of the Ryu): Shinan awarded this title to his son, Antonio Pereira Jr. But his son, who was a Judo practitioner and not Miyama Ryu, for personal reasons, declined active involvement in the Ryu. For this reason this title is not utilized by Miyama Ryu practitioners.

Executive Boards

For purposes of grading or organization a Dai-Shihan may form a local or regional Executive Board comprised of his choosing. This board will act in an advisory capacity and has no decision making capacity except that given by the Dai-Shihan who formed it. Each Dai Shihan is his own authority on all matters concerning the Ryu except changes to the core curriculum and appointment of other Dai-Shihans. In these cases an International Executive Board comprised of all Dai-Shihans will make the decisions.

Approved Instructor

An approved instructor is an instructor operating under the auspices of a Dai-Shihan. An approved instructor can be any rank provided a Dai-Shihan has given permission for the classes. Approved Instructors certification should be renewed each year by a Dai-Shihan.

Promotion rights of an Approved Instructor

Mudansha - NONE. Arrangement shall be made through a Dai-Shihan.

Okuiri - Up to and including Nikyu (2nd kyu).

Mokuroku - Up to and including Ikkyu (1st kyu).

Menkyo – Up to and including Ikkyu (1st kyu). Additionally a Menkyo may be authorized by a Dai-Shihan to grade up to and including Okuiri. The promotion must be submitted to a Dai-Shihan for signature.

Kaiden - Up to and including Ikkyu. Additionally, a Kaiden may be authorized by a Dai-Shihan to grade up to and including Mokuroku. The promotion must be submitted to a Dai-Shihan for signature.

Special Note: All grades above Mokuroku must be made in person by a Dai-Shihan. All certificates of the grades (Okuiri through Kaiden) must be signed by a Dai-Shihan or the rank is not a valid Miyama Ryu Rank

In the Event of the Retirement or Death of a Dai-Shihan

In the event of the retirement or death of a Dai-Shihan another Dai-Shihan can be appointed if the remaining Dai-Shihans are in agreement, until this decision the most senior Kaiden/Shihan will immediately occupy this position.

Index

A

A talk with Shinan Pereira 17
About the Author 6
Atemi Waza (striking) 45
Attitude in the Dojo 22
Attitude in training 23
Attitude of the Tori 24
Attitude of the Uke 26

B

Belt Tests and Promotion Requirements 175
Body Grabs from Behind 82,109, 110, 142

C

Club Attacks 87, 115, 116, 157 - 159

F

Foreword 7
Formal Bow 58
Formal Moves 90 – 92, 118, 119, 163 - 167
Front Body Grabs 143 - 146
Front Chokes 160, 1612

H

History of Combat Jujutsu 12
History of Miyama Ryu 15

I

Introduction 9

K

Kamae (posture and attitude) 39
Kansetsu waza (joint locking) 47
Kansetsuwaza 76, 132, 133

Kiai Jutsu (the spirit shout) 40
Knife Attacks 85, 86, 114, 153, 154
Kote Waza(wrist locking) 46
Kotegaeshi (Right & Left) 70 - 72, 100, 131
Kyusho (Targeting) 52

L

Lapel Grabs 79, 80, 137, 140
Lineage chart 11

M

Maai (Combative Distance) 55
Miyama Ryu Heiho (strategy and tactics) 10
Mugs 83, 84, 112, 148
Multiple Attack 150 -152
Multiple Attacks 30

N

Nage Waza (throwing)   49

O

Owaza (the complete technique) 42

P

Promotion requirements for 6th Kyu Green Belt 124
Promotion requirements for 6th Kyu Orange Belt   57
Promotion requirements for 6th Kyu Yellow Belt   95

R

Rank and Promotion Procedures 184

S

Safety in the Dojo 32
Shime Waza (strangulation) 51
Sport? 33

T

Tai sabaki (body positioning) 44
Taisabaki 62 -69, 129
Taiso (body positioning) 34
Timing 56

U

Ukemi (break falls) 43
Ukemi 61, 126 - 127
Unarmed Attacks 28

W

Weapon Attacks 29
Wrist Grabs 74 -77, 102-104, 135

Dynamic Seminars with Dai Shihan D'Arcy Rahming
www.miyamaryu.org
"The bad guys have a plan. What's yours?"

Let the world's foremost authority on Miyama Ryu help you to take your organization to the next level and beyond. Dai Shihan D'Arcy Rahming is an internationally sought after seminar leader and motivational speaker who has taught and inspired thousands of individuals world wide. Contact us today at *info@miyamaryu.org* to find out how Dai Shihan Rahming can help you develop your plan of action.

Certified seminars available in:

Miyama Ryu Combat Jujutsu
Tanjo jutsu (Walking stick)
Ju jo (Flexible stick)
Self-defense
Women's self–defense
Self-defense for college students
Police and Security Specialist Defensive Tactics
OC Pepper Spray
Work Place Violence
Non violence for grade school, junior high and high school students

Introducing the Secrets of Combat Jujutsu Series
www.miyamaryu.org

Secrets of Combat Jujutsu Vol. I, 3rd Edition

Learn the self-defense techniques and philosophies of the Samurai updated for today's tough streets. Over 700 illustrations demonstrate 125 White through Green Belt Combat Jujutsu techniques. Book contains 192 pages.

List Price: $24.95

1-886219-07-9

Secrets of Advanced Combat Jujutsu Vol. II, 3rd Edition

The advanced textbook of Samurai self-defense techniques and philosophies updated for today's tough streets. Over 1000 illustrations demonstrate 150 lessons of Brown Belt Combat Jujutsu techniques. Book contains 240 pages.

List Price $ 29.95

1-886219-08-7

Secrets of Black Belt Combat Jujutsu Vol. III, 2nd Edition

The Black Belt textbook of Samurai self-defense techniques and philosophies updated for today's tough streets. Over 1200 illustrations demonstrate 200 lessons of Black Belt Combat Jujutsu techniques. Book contains 256 pages.

List Price $ 29.95

1-886219-09-5

Koryu Online:

The internet Resource of the Classical Martial Arts

http://www.koryu.com

A unique compendium of photographs, essays, excerpts, book reviews, and more. Visit today and take advantage of the wealth of free information we have collected, and keep up-to-date on the latest Koryu Books publications. If you'd like to read more quality books like this one, check out our special online bookstore, where you can read detailed reviews of our selected recommendations, then order any title for immediate shipment. Your satisfaction with your purchase is 100% guaranteed or your money will be cheerfully refunded.

Made in the USA
Columbia, SC
28 December 2018